Alexander Hutton Drysdale

The English Presbyterians

a historical handbook of their rise, decline, and revival

Alexander Hutton Drysdale

The English Presbyterians
a historical handbook of their rise, decline, and revival

ISBN/EAN: 9783337092207

Printed in Europe, USA, Canada, Australia, Japan

Cover: Foto ©ninafisch / pixelio.de

More available books at **www.hansebooks.com**

THE
ENGLISH PRESBYTERIANS

A HISTORICAL HANDBOOK

OF THEIR

RISE, DECLINE, AND REVIVAL

BY

REV. A. H. DRYSDALE, M.A.

AUTHOR OF THE "HISTORY OF THE PRESBYTERIANS IN ENGLAND," "EARLY
BIBLE SONGS," "ST. PAUL'S EPISTLE TO PHILEMON," &c.

LONDON

PUBLISHING OFFICE OF THE

PRESBYTERIAN CHURCH OF ENGLAND

14 PATERNOSTER SQUARE

1891

PREFACE.

THIS Handbook is issued at the request of the Presbyterian Church of England's Committee on the "Higher Instruction of Youth," and in connection with part of their work. It is for substance an epitome of the Author's larger volume. The writer is alone responsible for what the book contains; but he has had the advantage of suggestions from some members of Committee who have kindly looked over the proofs; and he would fondly hope the manual may serve not mere denominational purposes but higher Christian interests as well.

CONTENTS.

INTRODUCTION.

Design of Handbook	13
Presbyterian Name in England	13
Meaning of Presbyterian	14
Presbyterian Elements traceable :	
In the Ancient British Church	15
In the Church of Northumbria	16
In the Anglo-Saxon Church	17
In the Mediæval Church	18
In Wycliffe and his Lollards	19
In the Ecclesiastical Revolution under Henry VIII.	20

PART I.

RISE OF THE PRESBYTERIANS IN THE REFORMED CHURCH OF ENGLAND.

CHAPTER I.—INCEPTIVE PERIOD, 1549-1559.

Martin Bucer's Proposals for further Church Reform to Edward VI., 1549-1551	22
John A'Lasco and his London Charter, 1550	23
John Hooper and the Priestly Vestments, 1551	24
John Knox and Presbyterian Worship in England, 1549-1553	25
The Marian Exiles in Geneva become Presbyterian, 1554-1559	26

Chapter II.—Formative Period, 1559-1582.

Early years of Elizabeth's Reign	28
Queen Elizabeth's Religious Policy	29
Development of a Presbyterian Party	30
The Presbyterian Leader—Thomas Cartwright	32
The Discipline and the Prophesyings	33
A Memorable Year	34
First Parochial Presbytery at Wandsworth, 1572	35
The First and Second Admonitions to Parliament, 1572	36
Growth and Spread of Presbyterian Views. The Directory	36
Presbyterianism Established in Jersey and Guernsey, 1576	37

Chapter III.—The Repressive Period, 1582-1602.

Suppression of the Prophesyings	38
The Grand Struggle	38
Subscribers to the Presbyterian Directory	39
The Mar-Prelate Controversy and Tracts	40
John Udall, the Presbyterian Martyr	41
Further Struggles and Persecutions	42

Chapter IV.—Period of the Irrepressible, 1603-1643.

Hampton Court Conference and the harryings, 1604-1625	44
New Soil for Presbyterian Growth, 1625-1637	45
Presbyterian Exiles and the British Synod in Holland	45
Presbyterian Pamphlets and Early Debates in the Long Parliament, 1641	46
Ejection of Bishops from House of Lords, 1642	46

Chapter V.—Period of Presbyterian Ascendency, 1643-1649.

Parliament calls the Westminster Assembly, and both Swear to the Covenant, 1643	48

Work of the Westminster Assembly	49
The Shorter Catechism	54
The Assembly's Brief Doctrinal Statement	55
Close of the Assembly	57
Presbyterian London, 1643-1649	57
Presbyterian Church Established in Lancashire, 1646	59
Presbyterianism in other Counties of England	59
English Presbyterians and their Work in America	60

PART II.
DECLINE OF THE PRESBYTERIANS IN ENGLAND.

CHAPTER I.—PERIOD OF DISAPPOINTMENT AND FAILURE, 1649-1662.

How the Presbyterians failed to Establish themselves	62
Charge of Intolerance alleged against them	63
Christopher Love, an English Presbyterian Covenanter and Martyr	64
The Presbyterians under the Commonwealth and Protectorate	65
Richard Baxter and his peculiar Influence	66
Presbyterianism in the Balance	67

CHAPTER II.—THE HEROIC PERIOD, 1662-1688.

Act of Uniformity, and Ejection of the Two Thousand, 1662	69
Their Sufferings and Persecution	70
The Lowest Depth	71
Philip Henry:	72
His Childhood	72
At Westminster School and Christ Church, Oxford	73
Ordained Minister at Worthenbury	73
The Ejected Presbyterian at Broad Oak	74
Presbyterian Puritanism: Its real Nature and Vitality	75

CHAPTER III.—TOLERATION AND MEETING-HOUSE BUILDING PERIOD, 1688-1710.

Toleration or Comprehension?	78
The Celebrated "Enquiry," 1691	79
The Early Presbyterian Meeting-Houses	79
Peculiarities of the New Presbyterian Position	80
"Happy Union" of Presbyterians and Independents, 1690-1694	81
Rupture of the Union in London. Dr. Daniel Williams and the Anti-nomian Controversy	82
Matthew Henry, the celebrated Commentator:	83
His Early Life	83
His Presbyterial Position and Ministry	83

CHAPTER IV.—TRANSITIONAL AND SPASMODIC PERIOD, 1710-1740.

Trying and Changing Influences at work, from 1710	85
The Subscription Controversy in Exeter Assembly and Salters' Hall, 1719	86
Dr. Edmund Calamy (born 1671, died 1732)	87
Insidious Tendency to Arianism, and its Causes, 1730-1760	87
Unhappy Predicament of the Presbyterians	88

CHAPTER V.—PERIOD OF DEFECTION AND DECAY, 1740-1800.

Depressed State of Religion in the Country	90
Nature and Drift of the Arian Tendency, 1735-1780	91
Spiritual Decay and Presbyterian Decrease	92
Arianism driven to Unitarianism, 1780-1800	93

PART III.
REVIVAL OF THE PRESBYTERIANS IN ENGLAND.
CHAPTER I.—PRIMARY PERIOD, 1672-1820.

Sources of the Revival	94
First Scottish Presbyterian Churches in England	95

Scottish Secession Churches in England 95
Faithful Remnant of English Presbyterian Congregations ... 96
Presbyterian Survival in the Northern Counties, especially in
Northumberland 97

CHAPTER II.—PERIOD OF METHODIST DEVELOPMENT,
1735-1890.

How Methodism under Wesley became Presbyterian 99
   John Wesley a Presbyterian 99
   Wesley's Methodism a Presbyterian Church 100
Rise of the Calvinistic Methodist or Presbyterian Church in
Wales 100
   The Spiritual Awakening, 1735 and 1791 101
   The Presbyterian Organisation, 1811-1864 101

CHAPTER III.—PERIOD OF PRESBYTERIAL AND SYNODICAL
ORGANISATION, 1820-1843.

Evangelical Presbyterianism Organising itself: 103
   In Connection with the Scottish Secession 103
   In Connection with the National Church of Scotland ... 104
An English Synod formed in connection with the Church of
Scotland, 1836-1842 104
Favouring Circumstances : 105
   *Evangelical Presbyterians in the "General Body" of
   the Three Denominations* 105
   *Final Decision by the House of Lords in the Case of
   the Lady Hewley Trust, 1842* 105
   The Fluctuations of Unitarianism 106

CHAPTER IV.—PERIOD OF QUICKENING AND INCREASE,
1843-1846.

Fresh Impulses in 1843 and 1847 107
The Presbyterian Church in England, as constituted in 1843 ... 108

William C. Burns and its China Mission, 1847 108
The United Presbyterian Church (1847), and its English Synod
(1867) 110
Causes of Presbyterian Separation 110
Dr. James Hamilton, and movements for Union 111

CHAPTER V.—PERIOD OF CONSOLIDATION AND EXTENSION,
1876-1891.

The Union of 1876, and the Presbyterian Church of England
constituted 112
The Presbyterian Church of England: 112
    Its Constitution 113
    Its Polity and Administration 114
    Its Doctrine 115
    Its Worship 116
    Its General Work 117
    Sustentation Fund 118
    Missions 118
    Education and Educational Work 120
    Its Growth and Position 121
Vast Extent of Presbyterianism. The Presbyterian General
Alliance 121
Conclusion 122

INTRODUCTION.

DESIGN OF HANDBOOK.—It is proposed here to tell the story of the Presbyterians in England, their Rise, Decline and Revival. The aim is a sectional but not a sectarian history. Presbyterians have played no slight nor unworthy part in the world at large, but in England their fortunes have been singularly chequered and their annals too often misunderstood. Thus by writers of England's *secular* history the Presbyterians are brought too suddenly to the surface in the days of their triumph, 1640-1660, and disappear no less suddenly without any explanation. In *ecclesiastical* annals, again, they usually figure as a mere sect or defeated faction in Church and State, without any hint of their great services to the country, or the world-wide results of their work.

PRESBYTERIAN NAME IN ENGLAND.—"Things are always ancienter than their names," says Richard Hooker. There were Reformers before the Reformation. There were Christians before "the disciples were first *called* Christians at Antioch". So there were Presbyterians long before the *word* Presbyterian was heard of. It began to be used in England about 1573, as a name for those who desired further reformation in the worship, discipline and government of the Church. They were also called "Precisians," or the "precise folk," because they wished to put away out of the Church everything not sanctioned by Scripture. But the name by which they were best known was "Puritans," because they wished to have the Church made Scripturally "pure" in its discipline and in all its usages. This was originally a nick-name, given them in 1564, which they resented at first as a party-title, though they had no reason afterwards to be ashamed of it. The earlier Puritans were practically the same as the Presbyterians. Others, who sprang up later and withdrew from the Church of England, were called "Separatists" or "Sectaries"; these chiefly held Independent or Baptist opinions. But the Presbyterian Puritans struggled on inside the National Church seeking further improvements; and when at last ejected with others in 1662 they carried on their work *outside*, and have done so ever since.

MEANING OF PRESBYTERIAN.—In answer to the question, What is the New Testament way of governing the Church? Presbyterians hold that as in the New Testament presbyters, elders, and bishops are only different titles for the same order of rulers, to whom the government of the Church was entrusted, it should be so still. Presbyterianism, therefore, is the system of Church government by bishops consulting together, and its three leading features are:—

1. That there is no higher kind of bishop by Divine authority than the bishops of a congregation. Of these bishops the minister is chosen not merely to rule, but to preach and preside in the Church as a pastor.

2. Church government is not to be exercised by one person, nor directly by the members at large, but by a body, or senate, or council of elders or bishops chosen for that purpose by the members of the Church. We never

read in the New Testament of a single elder or bishop, but *always* of elders or bishops in *every* Church;—elders or bishops *in the plural*, as well as deacons.

3. Originally when a church grew too large to meet together in one place, and had to be divided into several churches, these were not wholly severed, but remained *organically connected*, not, however, by one great bishop being placed over all, but by a common council or synod of elders or bishops acting together in brotherly fellowship. This is *representative* government, and Presbyterians have always struggled for it in the government of the Church as well as of the State. It is by this kind of council that both ministers and congregations are to be *superintended*, and not by a *bishop of bishops*, of which as a personal office Scripture says nothing. All believe there were bishops in the Church from the beginning, but the question is, What kind of bishops? not bishops of bishops, but bishops of the flock. Presbyterians believe in *Apostolic Episcopacy;* they reject, however, the idea of sacerdotal orders, but hold that the Church should possess a threefold ministry of DOCTRINE, DISCIPLINE, and DISTRIBUTION OF FUNDS, entrusted to office-bearers elected by her members.

There can hardly be said to have been a time since the introduction of Christianity into this country when one or other of these Presbyterian principles has not been held, or exemplified more or less in the Church. Let us trace some of these Presbyterian Elements.

IN THE ANCIENT BRITISH CHURCH.—Notwithstanding many early traditions and legends, like that about Joseph of Arimathæa and the holy thorn at Glastonbury, none can tell exactly when or how the Gospel came first to our island. Probably it was brought soon after Apostolic days by Christian Roman soldiers, and also by merchants from the East who visited parts of our shores beyond the Roman occupation. There were of course no cathedrals, dioceses, or prelates in those days, nor for centuries afterwards. A bishop then was simply a travelling preacher of the Gospel sent forth from some missionary or collegiate institute (called afterwards by mistake a monastery), or he was the pastor of some humble church, built of clay and wattles, or he resided with some chief and his tribe as their Gospel missionary. Bishops of this latter kind were very numerous among the early British, Irish and Welsh tribes. After the Roman armies withdrew, the Saxons and Angles invaded our island; and, being savage heathen and idolaters, they burned and destroyed the Christian places of worship, and drove the British Church into mere corners of the country. It was in A.D. 595 that Gregory, bishop of Rome, sent Augustine, the monk (who must be distinguished from the great Augustine of Hippo, in Africa, two centuries earlier), to convert England again to the Christian faith. This was the first great missionary work of the Church of Rome outside the pale of the Latin-speaking peoples.

IN THE CHURCH OF NORTHUMBRIA.—The Angles of the old kingdom of Northumbria were not, however, converted under Romish influence, and rather resented Romish usurpation. They derived their church government and institutions from the old British or Celtic Church of Scotland, which sent the Gospel to them first. For when the famous Oswald, after a great victory, became *Bretwald* or *High Sovereign* from the Humber to the Forth, joining Britons, Picts, and Scots with Anglians under his sway, and when he eagerly desired the Gospel for his subjects, instead of looking southward to the Romish priesthood, he sent for missionaries from the grand old Church of Iona, in which he had himself been trained and baptised. "He sent to the elders of the Scots," says Venerable Bede, and obtained as the Apostle of Northumbria, the preacher AIDAN, who chose the island of Lindisfarne for the seat of his missionary institute, within sight of Bamborough, Oswald's royal residence, and so it became "Holy Island," or the Northumbrian Iona. "It was a touching thing," says Bede, "to see King Oswald, who had learned the Celtic tongue in his exile, interpreting and translating as Aidan preached." And he adds: "From that time many from the region of the Scots came daily into these parts, and with great devotion preached the word of faith to those provinces of the Angles over which King Oswald ruled". Thus did the old kingdom of Northumbria receive the Gospel from Scotland, A.D. 635.

IN THE ANGLO-SAXON CHURCH.—It would take long to tell how the Church of Rome in the South of England, and the Church of Iona in Northumbria came into collision at the Synod of Whitby, A.D. 664, and how at it the former gained one of its greatest triumphs. The famous historian Neander says: "Had the Scottish tendency prevailed, England would have maintained a more free Church Constitution; and a reaction against the Romish hierarchical system would have ever continued to go forth from this quarter". It is well to remember that such holy Celtic missionaries as St. COLUMBA of Scotland, St. PATRICK of Ireland, and St. AIDAN of England never belonged to the Romish Church, though *afterwards* she made them *Saints* for her own advantage. But although the Church of Rome then gained the ascendency in England, it required much time and pains to get her system fully established in the hands of bishops and clergy subject to the Pope. Not till near the end of the seventh century were either parishes or dioceses heard of in England. They were introduced chiefly by the Greek monk THEODORE of Tarsus, a layman whom the Pope had consecrated as primate among the Angles. But Church affairs were managed still by Synods or Councils, which met twice a year; and interesting records of many of them have come down to us. The principal thing to keep in mind about those synods is that both "clergy and laity" were associated and took part together in their proceedings, just as in our own presbyteries or synods. In fact, no such thing as a synod or convocation of clergy alone, without laymen, was heard of in England till long after the Norman Conquest, A.D. 1250. The early Saxon arrangements of the *Tithing*, the *Hundred or Shiremote*, and the *Wittenagemote* or *Assembly of the Wise* look to us wonderfully Presbyterian, and though there were presiding bishops in the Church they were very different from what they afterwards became —diocesan or Lord Bishops. So late as A.D. 994 we find the famous AELFRIC, in a very important document, declaring that the highest *order* in the Church is the Presbyter, who "hallows the housel" (consecrates the bread in the Lord's Supper) "and preaches to the people". It was this same Aelfric who testified so strongly against the doctrine of transubstantiation, then beginning to prevail with other corruptions.

IN THE MEDIÆVAL CHURCH.—Although during the middle ages, the Prelatic and Papal Church system reigned supreme, it would be easy to mention the names of great and good men, like ANSELM Archbishop of Canterbury (A.D. 1093), GRATIAN, the great authority on Canon Law, PETER LOMBARD, the renowned theological oracle, (who both flourished in the twelfth century), and others, who knew and taught from Scripture that the prevailing church arrangements were merely of human institution; that bishops should not think themselves a different *order* of ministers from Presbyters, because they were both really one by *Apostolic appointment*, and that the Church was originally governed by the common consent and counsel of Elders.

But these views were most clearly brought to light and exemplified:—

IN WYCLIFFE AND HIS LOLLARDS, 1380-1400.—It is almost impossible to speak too highly of JOHN WYCLIFFE, the "Morning Star of the Reformation," who was also the truest of patriots, the first of English Bible translators, and the most devoted of Christian labourers. He is by far the grandest figure of his time in England, and the noblest of reformers before the Reformation. Happily his influence is not exhausted. It is growing still. Many of John Wycliffe's writings are only now being printed for the first time. They show that he was a Puritan before the Puritans, and a Presbyterian before the Presbyterians. For the movement under Wycliffe was a revolt not only against the corrupt doctrine, morals and worship of the Church, but against its unscriptural constitution and government as well. According to an old authority, John Wycliffe first struck the living spark of a revived Gospel: John Huss, his disciple in Bohemia, blew it into a flame, and then Luther bore aloft the blazing light. The Bible was Wycliffe's one and only standard. And very dear it was to him. By long and prayerful study of it, he was led by the Spirit of God to clear and consistent views of its teaching about the Church. The Apostles, he said, knew no such dignitaries as Pope or Prelate. Bishops and Presbyters were identical in Scripture. Priests who did not preach were an invention of the devil, and a mere mockery of the Christian ministry. And so he was led at last to denounce the whole hierarchical and prelatical system, as well as the positive blasphemy of the Papal claims. Nor did his work cease with denunciation, for he began to give practical effect to his views by training and sending forth his "poor priests" or "Bible-men," to preach and evangelise. Wycliffe loved the Gospel in its simplicity and purity. And the great schism in the Papacy, lasting nearly forty years after 1378, when the two rival Popes Urban VI. and Clement VII. cursed and excommunicated each other, afforded a grand and providential means of protection for Wycliffe and his Lollard preachers. Vengeance could only be wreaked afterwards on his bones. But by the fierce action of the Bishops the frightful enactment to "*burn heretics*" was at length passed in the English Parliament of 1401. Then began such havoc against the Lollard movement that it was finally stamped out in blood and fire, William Sautree, William Thorpe, and Sir John Oldcastle (Lord Cobham), being among the most prominent of its martyrs.

IN THE ECCLESIASTICAL REVOLUTION UNDER HENRY VIII.—In England, as elsewhere, the Reformation had two aspects. As an outward ecclesiastical movement it was an insurrection against the rule of the Pope; as an inward religious revival it was a resurrection of the rule of God's own Word. What Henry VIII. promoted was not the religious revival, but the great revolt from the authority of Rome. What he did was to wrench England from the Papal power, so as himself to become Pope, or "Supreme Head" of the English Church. He also totally suppressed the monasteries, and by the removal of all abbots from the House of Peers he greatly weakened the power of the prelates in the State. Henry had, however, first of all adroitly secured what is known as "the submission of the clergy," and in a very remarkable book, *The Institution of a Christian Man*, he caused the archbishops and a number of bishops and other authorities to teach that in the New Testament there is no mention but of two Orders, that of deacons and that of presbyters or bishops, and all power of one bishop over another is from man only, and not by any ordinance of God in Holy Scripture. This had also been taught in the *Practice of Prelates* by WILLIAM TYNDALE—the greatest of all our English Bible translators, and the foremost of Gospel teachers, who was burned at the stake as a martyr, crying, "Lord, open the eyes of the King of England".

PART I.

RISE OF THE PRESBYTERIANS IN THE REFORMED CHURCH OF ENGLAND.

CHAPTER I.

INCEPTIVE PERIOD, 1549-1559.

MARTIN BUCER'S PROPOSALS FOR FURTHER CHURCH REFORM.—When young Edward VI. succeeded his father the Reformation went forward apace. Many foreign divines were invited by royal authority to come and help in the work. Among the most distinguished and most heartily welcomed were Martin Bucer and John A'Lasco. Their writings are of special value in throwing light on those strong and more Presbyterian forms of Protestantism which the Reformation under Edward VI. tended to assume. Both were often consulted by Lord Protector Somerset, Cranmer, and other chief councillors, and they exercised no small influence on the opinions and procedure of the young king and his advisers. They were both Presbyterian (though not *called* so at the time), and it was largely through them that the SECOND English Prayer Book in 1552 was by far the most Protestant edition that has ever been issued. Just before his death Martin Bucer or Kuhorn (who had been made Divinity Professor at Cambridge, as his Italian friend Vermigli or Peter Martyr had been made at Oxford) prepared in Latin for the use of Edward VI. a wonderful little treatise, *On the Kingdom of Christ*, containing an outline of a more Scriptural and Presbyterian form of government, which greatly delighted the young king, as appears from the writings and remains of Edward VI., which have come down to us. The young king drew out with his own hand a project of church reform, according to its leading suggesttions for "reducing Episcopacy"; and only his early death in his sixteenth year, 1552, prevented some such scheme being attempted at that time.

JOHN A'LASCO AND HIS LONDON CHARTER.—The whole life of this remarkable man is of great interest. His London labours have special significance for us, founder as he was of the first legally recognised body of churches outside the National Church in England. These churches of his were organised on a Presbyterian plan. John A'Lasco, or, in his own native tongue, Laski, was a Polish nobleman, of high birth and ancient family, who might have been, like his uncle, the Primate or Archbishop of Poland, but for his becoming a Protestant and, better still, a humble follower of the meek and lowly Jesus. He endured many wanderings and hardships for Christ's and conscience' sake; but in England his great worth was recognised. At that time there were in London alone thousands of religious refugees, and by a great charter granted them by Edward VI. in 1550 these exiles were constituted the "Church of the Strangers," with A'Lasco as superintendent or chief pastor, and four other pastors as colleagues. There were two leading sections, the Germans in Austin Friars' Church, and the French in St. Anthony's, Threadneedle Street, but they had a common

" Sustentation " Fund, and regular meetings of all the elders and deacons. In a beautiful treatise addressed to the King of Poland, A'Lasco himself explains how Edward VI. and some of his Council designed to have a model to which the Church of England might be brought to conform when the mind of the people was ripe for it. All this of course came to an end when Mary succeeded to the throne. A'Lasco returned to Poland to be its Chief Reformer, but he died, too soon for his country, in 1560. He left his mark there, however, as well as on those foreign Churches in London which now look back on a long and interesting line of history.

JOHN HOOPER AND THE PRIESTLY VESTMENTS.—This great London preacher, when nominated Bishop of Gloucester by Edward VI. in 1550, refused to wear some parts of the priestly garb at his consecration. Strange! that a question of dress should play so prominent a part in English Church Reform. Yet not without reason. For the white surplice and other official garments were understood to be sacerdotal or priestly attire, declaring a real Christian priesthood to belong only to the clergy. Hence by the sure instinct that sees loyalty or disloyalty in the colour of a flag, and that determines the side a soldier is on by the uniform he wears, did both parties fasten on the vestments question as vital. Rather than wear them as a bishop, Hooper went even to prison. Is a minister of the Gospel a *priest*, or is he a *preacher?* Has he to stand between God and the people, making their peace with Heaven and offering a sacrifice for their sins at an altar, or has he simply to teach them the truth as it is in Jesus, and enforce it on their hearts and consciences? These were the two views of the Christian Ministry then struggling together for a foothold in the Church of England. This it was that forced on at length the other great question, How best to govern the Church and administer its affairs.

The people had been long accustomed to think of Christ's ministers as a sacrificing priesthood, dealing with God for them rather than speaking for God to them. This is still a great and vital question of serious moment. Nicholas Ridley, Bishop of London, who had been busy, along with others, in pulling down altars in the churches, and who was yet willing to use the surplice and vestments as things indifferent, was sent to argue with Hooper, but in vain. At length the King and his Council met Hooper half way: but the great question of the vestments was to mingle with the whole Puritan struggle which Hooper so clearly foresaw and so firmly supported.

JOHN KNOX AND PRESBYTERIAN WORSHIP IN ENGLAND.—Having been set free from the French galleys through the appeals of Edward VI. and his Council, John Knox, who was yet to be the great Reformer of Scotland, devoted five of his best years to their service in England, 1549-1553. He was one of the eighty travelling or circuit preachers specially licensed and appointed to evangelise in different centres throughout the kingdom. He spent two years in Berwick, two in Newcastle, and one about London, when he was also a royal chaplain, preaching to the King and carrying the Gospel with great effect to all places around.

The "Mass" Knox always denounced as "idolatry," because the people bowed in worship before the "host," or consecrated wafer of bread, as if it had been changed into the real body of Christ. He taught the people to receive the Lord's Supper sitting as at a table, and not kneeling as if the Lord's table were an altar. And when the authorities of the English Church ordained kneeling at the Communion, it was Knox who got them to declare in the Second Prayer Book that no adoration was thereby intended to any supposed presence of Christ's body in the bread or wine.

This has been called the *Black Rubric* ever since by those who do not like it.

John Knox, who has been called "the grandest figure in the entire history of the British Reformation," declined to be made a diocesan bishop: Hooper accepted a bishopric on certain conditions. This was almost the only difference between these two thorough-going Reformers. But Hooper began to give a new idea of what a bishop should be, and some of the most distinctive Presbyterian and Puritan watchwords are to be found in Hooper's as much as in Knox's writings. When Edward VI. died, and "bloody Mary" came to the throne, Knox escaped to the Continent, but Hooper was reserved for the martyr-fire. "We have been two in white, let us be one in red," wrote Ridley to him, when they were both in prison. They had been divided formerly about the white surplice: now they were to be united in the fiery-red robe of the martyr's flame. Hooper's sufferings at Gloucester were of exceptional barbarity, and the story of them is a very touching one, which all should seek out and read.

THE MARIAN EXILES IN GENEVA BECOME PRESBYTERIAN. —While the fires of persecution were blazing as they had never before done in England, during the five years of Mary's miserable reign from 1553 to 1558, hundreds of eminent English Protestants escaped to the Continent. They were made especially welcome among THE REFORMED CHURCHES of Germany and Switzerland, and as these Reformed Churches were already Presbyterian in worship and government, many of the English exiles learned to prefer that way, and they thus became more Presbyterian than before. This was particularly the case with those who found shelter in the free imperial city of Frankfort-on-Main, and afterwards in Geneva. Owing to troubles and differences in the former town the Presbyterian plan was never fully carried out there, although a Book of Order had been prepared. It was at Geneva, therefore, that the FIRST ENGLISH PRESBYTERIAN CHURCH was set up, 1551. And a remarkable church it was—John Knox, who had officiated at Frankfort, being again chosen chief minister and moderator, with Christopher Goodman and Anthony Gilby as his colleagues; while men like Whittingham, Sampson, and Miles Coverdale who had just been Bishop of Exeter, did not disdain to act as fellow-elders. They had brought with them from Frankfort the *Book of Common Order*, or Book of Geneva (commonly called Knox's Liturgy), which had, however, been composed chiefly by WILLIAM WHITTINGHAM, Calvin's brother-in-law, who was afterwards Dean of Durham, though he was never episcopally ordained, and by JOHN FOXE, who was yet to write his famous *Book of Martyrs*, which did so much to strengthen Protestant feeling in England in years to come. But the work of highest importance produced by these exiles was their English translation of Holy Scripture, which was so long the *popular* English version, the GENEVA BIBLE of 1560, with its pithy notes and the division of the text into *verses*. MILES COVERDALE, the venerable helper of Tyndale in his translations, took a leading part in this work.

CHAPTER II.

Formative Period, 1559-1582.

EARLY YEARS OF ELIZABETH'S REIGN.—When Elizabeth came to the throne, 17th November, 1558, the advanced Reformers hoped for very thorough purging of the Church. The new Queen was a Protestant, but, as the result showed, rather on political than on religious grounds. She was very fond of power. Neither pope nor people must dictate to her. Among the most memorable Acts of her first Parliament were THE ACT OF SUPREMACY, which gave her power *over* the Church, and THE ACT OF UNIFORMITY, which gave her extraordinary power *within* it. From the Royal Commissioners whom she appointed to carry out these two Acts there sprang the new COURT OF HIGH COMMISSION, which, with the older STAR CHAMBER COURT, enabled her to manage things very much as she liked both in Church and State.

She had great difficulty in getting bishops to her mind. When she had, after one failure, selected Matthew Parker in 1559 to be the first Protestant Archbishop of Canterbury, not one of the bishops of any English See would take part in consecrating him, as no one had ever been made archbishop of this diocese without permission of the Pope. Parker was inducted, therefore, into episcopal office by *four deprived bishops* of Edward VI.'s time; and one of them, *Miles Coverdale*, did duty in his *Geneva* cloak, or black gown, having been recently one of John Knox's own elders. Elizabeth would not restore him, however, to his bishopric at Exeter, and the bishops she appointed were far more Puritan and Protestant than she herself liked, the main body of them being at first both " *Calvinists in doctrine and inclined to Presbyterianism in discipline*," and much opposed to her own mongrel faith and semi-popish worship. How she changed them we shall afterwards see.

QUEEN ELIZABETH'S RELIGIOUS POLICY.—So great were the dangers and difficulties of Queen Elizabeth's position at first that the Act of Uniformity could not be rigorously enforced for some years. The Roman Catholics were still the most numerous and influential party in the kingdom, so that she had to proceed at the outset with great caution and even slowness in her measures. While the new Church settlement was under consideration very considerable freedom and latitude had for the same reason to be extended to the small but vigorous party of the Church Puritans, who from their zeal were not only increasing in numbers, but in many ways securing very decided advantages. Indeed, for a time it seemed impossible to say whether the Church of England might not become a Reformed Presbyterian Church altogether, like sister churches on the Continent; for the influence of the name of Calvin was very strong at that time in England. His " Institutes " was the theological text-book at the Universities, and all the English divines were Calvinists in their belief. The more advanced reformers were very well satisfied so far as concerned the *doctrine*, which had been drawn out and settled in the Church. But their strongest objections had reference to certain dangerous, and, as they thought, very unscriptural elements in the style of its *worship*. They struggled hard to have this remedied.

The high ritual and ceremonies, however, which they most disliked were the very things which the Queen delighted in, and to which she attached the greatest importance. And as she began to feel firmer on the throne she became more resolved to stamp out all who were opposed to her in this respect. She compelled her Bishops to do her bidding, however unwilling they were; and no one has left a deeper mark of personal influence on the Church of England than Queen Elizabeth. Having, however, little insight into *spiritual* Christianity, she had little sympathy with anything designed to promote it. Her own religion was far too much one of outward pomp and ceremony. She was, moreover, not unpractised in deceit, and even in profane swearing; and she had certain other not very estimable traits of character and moral weaknesses. In politics she managed things very well, for she was not only very able herself, but knew how to choose able and wise counsellors. In Church matters, however, she managed things very ill, for she would not be advised in them at all, though there she needed advice the most. Strong rule was necessary no doubt at the time, but her government would have been all the stronger had she been less self-willed, especially in matters of religion.

DEVELOPMENT OF A PRESBYTERIAN PARTY, 1562-1569.—In the year 1566 Elizabeth began to insist with new rigour on minute conformity to the habits and ceremonies of worship, especially in London and near the Court. Large numbers of the best ministers, like John Foxe and Miles Coverdale, were cast out of their livings because they could not comply with the Queen's requirements. At this time, a congregation of these persecuted Puritans set up secretly the Presbyterian worship and order in London, according to the Book of Geneva: and these were the first *separatists*, as they were called, from the English Church. They were not, however, very numerous nor influential, and were soon broken up by the Government. John Knox in Scotland and the leading reformers on the Continent disapproved of their separation; and all the chief sufferers in England, like Gilby, Goodman, Dr. William Turner, Lever (the Queen's own favourite preacher), Sampson, Humphrey, and many other distinguished men, resolved still to continue their efforts inside the Church for further reform. Many of them, however, began to see that the cause of the evils they deplored lay deeper down in the very constitution of the Church than they had at first thought: and that changes were needed in its government and management before they would be able to secure the reforms they desired. These were the Church Puritans who after a few years were known by the name of Presbyterians. When the great Popish rebellion of the northern nobles was suppressed in 1569, and the Queen felt her throne secure, she began to act more severely than ever in Church affairs: and this it was that did so much to compel the "more resolved" Puritans to look carefully into the foundation of Church government and the New Testament method of Church administration. For the first ten years of Elizabeth's reign the Puritans had struggled and suffered chiefly for the changes they desired in the Prayer Book. But by 1570 it was the Presbyterians who had come to the front, and during the next ten years they were laying down their plans and principles. The third period of her reign, from 1580 to 1588, was the time of their most arduous practical struggle; while during the fourth and last period after 1588, when the defeat of the Armada clothed Elizabeth with fresh glory and security, she showed herself so inflexibly severe in her ecclesiastical regulations that her popularity diminished as her power increased. This general view of Elizabeth's reign will enable us the better to understand the nature and aims of the Presbyterian movement, and the struggles and sufferings of the Presbyterian Puritans.

THE PRESBYTERIAN LEADER, THOMAS CARTWRIGHT.— Great movements generally centre round some great name. The young and rising Presbyterian party found a distinguished leader in THOMAS CARTWRIGHT. The more we know of this man the more highly we must think of him, yet he has been sadly misunderstood and abused, both in his own day and since. Born in Hertfordshire in 1535, he became one of the best students at Cambridge, and was advanced to the high post of Lady Margaret Professor of Divinity at the age of thirty-four. He was not only very able, learned, and eloquent, but his piety was intensely real and earnest. When he preached in St. Mary's the windows of the great church had to be removed, that the crowd outside might hear him. He spoke strongly against the abuses still remaining in the Church, and he feared that many superstitions and corruptions might creep into it again unless carefully guarded against. Among other things, he was shocked at the inequalities of office and income. Poor men, he said, did toil and travail, but great folks licked up all the profits. With his noble and fiery spirit, he hated and denounced mere outward shams and affectations in religion. In the service, for example, which is appointed in the Prayer Book for the first day of Lent people were taught to deplore the lack of the godly discipline which belonged to the primitive Church, and to wish it restored. They have been saying this for three centuries and more, but have done nothing to secure it! Cartwright would have had it done so long ago as 1570. He cried out for " the discipline," though all in vain. He wanted a spiritual eldership in the Church for spiritual purposes, and not mere political lawyers or legal officials to do the Church's work. Again, he felt the way of electing bishops to be a mere pretence, if not a profanation. Of course, he did not want bishops to be lords, nor ministers to be thought priests. Now, to please numbers who believed in priestly pretensions and Apostolic succession, Queen Elizabeth devised a way of seeming to allow the cathedral authorities to elect their bishop. She even required them to invoke the Holy Spirit to show them whom they should choose. But she always, in a letter, told them beforehand whom they *must* choose, under severe penalties if they disobeyed. And so, as the historian Froude has truly said, "the invocation of the Holy Spirit either meant nothing, and was a taking of sacred names in vain, or it implied that the Third Person of the Trinity was, as a matter of course, to register the already declared decision of the English Sovereign".

These and other evils, which we are sorry to say still exist, greatly stirred the mind of Cartwright. Holy Scripture, he maintained, should be the standard for the Church's *order and discipline* not less than for its *doctrine*. As Professor of Divinity, he began to show from the Acts of the Apostles what serious changes must be effected before the Church could be brought back to primitive and Apostolic usage. The lectures excited immense interest. Violent controversies, personal and political, arose, attended with extreme bitterness. Cartwright was hastily removed from his office, and retired to Geneva for a time. His friend BEZA declared: "Than Thomas Cartwright I think the sun doth not see a more learned man".

THE DISCIPLINE AND THE PROPHESYINGS.—Meanwhile Cartwright's Presbyterian ideas were taking root and spreading in England. Two watchwords, "THE DISCIPLINE" and "THE PROPHESYINGS," became familiar favourites with the young party. The discipline had special reference to purity of *communion* or *membership* in the Church, as distinguished from purity of *creed* or of *worship*. Out of this was to grow the parish eldership or parish Presbytery, while out of the prophesyings or exercises was to come the *Class* or district Presbytery, for the mutual edification and discipline of ministers and churches.

The first example of the eldership or parish Presbytery occurs at Wandsworth in 1572; and the first of the *Prophesyings* was set up at Northampton in 1571. Something of the same kind of discipline and ministerial fellowship had been previously established in the Church of the Strangers in London under John A'Lasco; and it was specially provided for in the *English Book of Order* which had been in use at Geneva. The object of "the Prophesyings" was to bring the teaching of Scripture to bear on the spiritual and moral experience of the people at large, and then to exercise the ministers themselves in godliness by their mutual dealings with one another in subsequently meeting as a Presbytery. The whole was thus a voluntary association for spiritual fellowship and discipline, and for the self-government both of ministers and people on Scriptural lines. The Prophesyings spread rapidly to other parts of the kingdom, and there was need for them, there being so many scandalous and worthless clergy, and the people themselves being so ignorant and godless. We shall see afterwards why the Queen was led to dislike and suppress these "Prophesyings".

A MEMORABLE YEAR.—The year 1572 is memorable in Presbyterian history. In FRANCE it was the year of the awful St. Bartholomew massacre of the Huguenots, or French Presbyterians. In HOLLAND it saw the commencement of the struggle which laid the foundation of the

Dutch Presbyterian Church. In SCOTLAND John Knox died and the *Tulchan* Bishops were set up: two disasters which, however, helped to lead the way at length to a Presbyterian triumph. In ENGLAND the year is specially noteworthy, for in it the Presbyterians took their first two great *practical* steps. They set up a Presbytery or parochial eldership, and they brought their scheme for Church reform under the notice of Parliament. Hitherto their programme existed only in theory; now it assumed a visible shape.

FIRST PAROCHIAL PRESBYTERY AT WANDSWORTH, 1572.—Presbyterians have always attached great importance to the Apostolic practice of appointing "elders in every church" (Acts xiv. 23). And so these early English Presbyterians were very anxious to have spiritual rule and discipline managed in each church by a Common Council of Elders, as at first. For it is in brotherly council, and not in the dictation of one man, be he pope, prelate, or parson, that Presbyterianism finds the key of both liberty and order, according to the Scriptures. A minister or bishop may preach and have special care of *doctrine*, but there must be a body of elders to watch over the flock and attend to its *discipline*. When, therefore, a number of earnest London ministers came together into an association, or CLASSIS, they resolved to begin their Church reform by ordaining a body of elders whom the godly people of the parish church of Wandsworth had chosen to assist their lecturer or preacher, JOHN FIELD, in his pastoral work. This was the first parochial Eldership, or PRESBYTERY, as they called it. We should now call it a *Church Session*, or lesser Presbytery. This lay at the root of the whole Presbyterian movement, and the little book or *Bill* called THE ORDER OF WANDSWORTH was meant as a guide or directory for establishing it in other parishes.

THE FIRST AND SECOND ADMONITIONS TO PARLIAMENT IN 1572.—All this work of discipline had to be gone about very quietly, even secretly. For if there were no law against it, there was yet no law to sanction it. The Presbyterians wished, however, to see it legalised, along with other changes in the Church. But having little or no hope from the Queen, their chief leaders, GILBY, SAMPSON, LEVER, and others, after much consultation, resolved on "An Admonition to Parliament," in which many noble patriots, like Strickland, Wentworth, Knollys, and others, were strongly on their side. They have been often foolishly blamed for calling it "an admonition," as if this implied some ecclesiastical rebuke or threat. This is a mistake, for "admonition" then meant merely a notice or intimation. The document is a very careful and elaborate paper, in twenty-three chapters—a full Presbyterian manifesto, showing clearly what was wanted in the Church. They knew that Parliament had, by law, equal rights with the Crown in this matter; for was not even the Queen's supremacy itself founded on an Act of Parliament? She was, however, dreadfully offended because Parliament had been asked to interfere. She seized the two London ministers who signed the document, JOHN FIELD and THOMAS WILCOX, and committed them to prison. At this juncture THOMAS CARTWRIGHT came back from the Continent, and not only defended his brethren, but even boldly wrote a "SECOND ADMONITION," and then had to flee abroad again for his very life.

GROWTH AND SPREAD OF PRESBYTERIAN VIEWS.—The controversy, however, continued to rage between CARTWRIGHT in exile and WHITGIFT, who afterwards became Archbishop of Canterbury. Many others took part in it, and WALTER TRAVERS, the learned colleague of Cartwright in the church at Antwerp, wrote in 1574 an elaborate Latin book to explain and defend the Presbyterian views. These two, CARTWRIGHT and TRAVERS, have been called, "the head and neck" of the movement, which, however, continued to develop and spread in England even in their absence. Whitgift did not answer Cartwright's "Second Reply"; twenty years later the gauntlet was taken up by Hooker in his famous "Ecclesiastical Polity". For ten years parochial presbyteries, classes or district presbyteries, and synods were held privately in many parts of the country, and at length, by 1583, the Great DIRECTORY of Church-government or Presbyterian Book of Discipline was ready, both in Latin and English. This was ultimately signed by 500 of the clergy of the Church of England, who strove to get it introduced and legalised for regulating the Church's government and discipline.

PRESBYTERIANISM ESTABLISHED IN JERSEY AND GUERNSEY.—Curiously enough, the Presbyterian form of government and worship had to be permitted and sanctioned by Queen Elizabeth, though very reluctantly, in the Channel Islands in 1576. For, being so near the French coast and using the French tongue, these islands had received their Protestant faith through Huguenot pastors and refugees. A French Reformed or Presbyterian Church had, therefore, become inevitable in Jersey and Guernsey. It continued to flourish for the next half century, until rudely disturbed by King James in 1625. Everywhere else, however, in her dominions Queen Elizabeth sought to uproot the Church Puritans or Presbyterians, although for political reasons she had to send armies to defend what was virtually the same cause in Holland and Scotland. Thus what she hated and repressed at home she supported as a matter of policy abroad.

CHAPTER III.

The Repressive Period, 1582-1602.

Suppression of the Prophesyings.—The first great blow to Presbyterian hopes in England was Elizabeth's edict of 7th May, 1577. Having no love for preaching (she thought one or two *preaching ministers* quite enough for a county), she feared the Prophesyings might lessen her power in the Church by introducing popular elements, and methods which were highly distasteful to her. After a most unseemly quarrel with Grindal, Archbishop of Canterbury, who wished, like other Puritan bishops and Privy Councillors, to retain these Prophesyings, she insisted on having them forcibly extinguished, and she succeeded in her purpose, greatly to the grief of her best Councillors and many even of her Bishops.

The Grand Struggle.—The great movement against the Presbyterians began, however, in 1583, when Whitgift succeeded Grindal as Archbishop. Two terrible measures he brought into operation: first, the Whitgift Articles, which, though in some points illegal, he yet used under royal prerogative to get rid of Presbyterian ministers; and second, the New High Commission, with powers to suspend, imprison, or eject all who would not submit. There were then many ministers of Presbyterian principles, and with Presbyterian ordination, who maintained they had a perfectly legal right to retain their places in the Church of England as it was at that time constituted by law. The two things for which they struggled were—(1) That the law, and not anyone's arbitrary will, should rule in the Church. The nation is everlastingly indebted to these Presbyterian Puritans for laying such stress upon this grand constitutional principle. (2) That Scripture should be the one supreme standard for the government, discipline, and officers of the Church, as well as for its doctrine and worship. It was in holding fast by these convictions, and in suffering for them, that the Presbyterians of those days became the anvil on which were struck forth the ever-brightening sparks of civil and religious liberty. A great ecclesiastical crisis was reached in 1584, when the House of Commons resolved to petition Her Majesty, but failed to receive the necessary consent of the Lords. They asked for thorough reforms— that Presbyters and Bishops should be on a level as to ordination; that no minister should be settled in a parish without being called by the people; that the Prophesyings be restored, and suspensions cancelled. The next ten years witnessed many a scene of persecution and imprisonment. Without a lawful and open trial before the courts, hundreds of Presbyterians were cast out of their parishes by what was called the EX-OFFICIO or inquisitorial oath, which compelled a man to be a witness against himself—a most unjust procedure—and shockingly illegal treatment was dealt out to them, as well as to the other kinds of Puritans who were now beginning to spring up. For unfortunately the Puritans were becoming divided among themselves, some breaking away from the Church altogether, and bitterly denouncing it as quite incapable of reform. These were called *sectaries* or *separatists*.

SUBSCRIBERS TO THE PRESBYTERIAN DIRECTORY.—The

Presbyterians continued their struggle, however, *within* the Church which they loved, and sought to spiritually amend. But although it is commonly understood that 500 clergy of the Church of England subscribed the Presbyterian Directory or Book of Discipline between 1583 and 1590, only a small proportion of their names can now be recovered. Some very notable men, however, were associated as subscribers with Cartwright, Travers, and their fellows. Among them were Divinity Professors and Heads of Colleges like Dr. JOHN RAINOLDS of Oxford, and Dr. WHITAKER, "the oracle of Cambridge," with his successor, Dr. LAWRENCE CHADDERTON; famous preachers and writers in practical religion like WILLIAM PERKINS and BRADSHAW; earnest clergy throughout the country like ARTHUR HILDERSHAM of Ashby de la Zouche, and HUMPHREY FENN of Coventry; and eminent sufferers like UDALL and CAWDREY. Many died under suspension or deprivation, like WILCOCKS and SNAPE; and others, like DUDLEY FENNER and the PAGETS, escaped abroad. A few even survived as links with the Divines who sat in the Westminster Assembly. Dr. Lawrence Chadderton had reached his 103rd year when he died in 1640. But the last of the survivors who "signed the Discipline" was the venerable JOHN DOD of Hanwell (commonly called the *Decalogist* from his work on the Ten Commandments), who did not die till 1645, aged 96, and who was thus a contemporary of the Westminster Assembly for two years. These Presbyterians all loved the Church, and struggled to reform it from within.

THE MAR-PRELATE CONTROVERSY AND TRACTS.—After the defeat of the Spanish Armada in 1588, when all fear of invasion was at an end, the authorities in Church and State became harsher and more savage in their treatment of these Church-Puritans. The bishops, or prelates as they were called, (that is bishops with *civil* lordship and jurisdiction) were specially distinguished for severity. Bishops in those days in England had prisons of their own, which they were not slow to use; while the Archbishop of Canterbury and the Bishop of London had command of all printing-presses, so that nothing could be issued without their special licence and permission. These interferences with civil liberty incensed multitudes and led to the publication of the Martin Marprelate tracts which were wrongly attributed to leading Presbyterian ministers. A *secret* printing-press kept moving about from place to place was at work on these fierce satires against the prelates. The tracts or pamphlets, forty or so in number, were very bitter, and they were answered by others equally virulent. No one knows who supplied the press with matter, but several sectaries were put to death on suspicion of being connected with it, and the Presbyterian cause also was made to suffer.

JOHN UDALL, THE PRESBYTERIAN MARTYR, 1592.—One of the most shocking illustrations of severity and illegal maltreatment toward the Presbyterians was the case of the pious and learned Rev. John Udall. He and the other Presbyterian leaders were greatly opposed to the violent spirit of the Mar-Prelate Tracts; but having himself issued from the same secret and unlicensed press (as was alleged) two very able treatises against Prelacy and in favour of Presbyterianism, he was tried and condemned to death for attacking the royal prerogative itself, because it was pretended that the bishops were part of the Queen's body politic. Arguing against them was, therefore, treason to her! The conviction of such a man on such grounds is, according to Hallam the historian, "one of the gross judicial iniquities of Elizabeth's reign"; while the trial, he says, "disgraces the name of English justice".

FURTHER STRUGGLES. — Meanwhile the Presbyterians strove hard for their cause in Parliament, in the High Commission and other courts, as well as from the pulpit and by pamphlets printed abroad; but all to little or no purpose. Their efforts to secure liberty and recognition for themselves in the Church were unavailing. Nay, the attacks on them grew fiercer as Elizabeth's reign went on; especially after 1590, when it was discovered how many ministers had signed the Presbyterian Directory, and how many "Classes" and parochial presbyteries were at work. These, it appears, were most fully organised in Northamptonshire, a suitable and central county, whence they spread to others. But all this quiet progress was now brought to a stop, not only through the prolonged imprisonment of Cartwright and many others by the High Commission and Star Chamber, but by Parliament consenting in a panic to pass the terrible law of 1593, one of the most shocking that ever sullied the statute-book of England, directed equally against the Separatists outside the Church and the Presbyterians within her pale, and intended by one fell stroke to extinguish both. Many now fled the country altogether, increasing numbers taking refuge in Holland and elsewhere. Presbyterianism was unmercifully struck down wherever it manifested itself, but its secret supporters were included among the partially conforming DOCTRINAL PURITANS (as they were called). Such were Rainolds, Perkins, Baynes, Bolton, with their successors, Dr. Preston and Dr. Richard Sibbes, who did so much by preaching and writing to maintain vital godliness among the people. They had, indeed, failed to gain all they wished for the Church, but they succeeded in making it far more Protestant than it would otherwise have been; while their inner meaning and spirit effected much good of even a higher kind—which has been beautifully interpreted in *The Faerie Queen* and other poems by their finest representative, Edmund Spenser, who pathetically bewailed the pomp of the Prelacy and other abuses derived from Rome and still retained in the Church of England.

CHAPTER IV.

Period of the Irrepressible, 1603-1643.

Hampton Court Conference and the Harryings, 1604-1625.—The Presbyterians are little heard of at the end of Queen Elizabeth's reign. They were compelled to be quiet. But, remembering the Presbyterian training and professions of King James, they had hopes of some consideration and favour on his accession in 1603. This looked the more likely when he summoned the Conference to meet at Hampton Court on the 14th January, 1604. He acceded readily to the suggestion of Dr. Rainolds for a new translation of Scripture, but he broke out violently at his suggestion to establish Presbytery in the memorable words: "Presbytery agreeth as well with monarchy as God and the devil. Let that government be once up, and we shall all have work enough and our hands full." From that moment his theologic and despotic wrath was kindled, and his closing words, as he shuffled out of the Conference, were: "I will make them conform or I will *harry* them out of the land". And he kept his word! A prominent sufferer who had "signed the discipline" was Arthur Hildersham, a divine of high birth and no less high character and attainment. He was of the Royal Tudor House, Queen Elizabeth herself greeting him as "Cousin Hildersham". Born in 1563 and living till 1632, he is one of the many links between the suffering Elizabethan Presbyterians and those of Charles I.'s time. Humphrey Fenn, John Dod, and Dr. Lawrence Chadderton, are other examples.

NEW SOIL FOR PRESBYTERIAN GROWTH, 1625-1637.— Prelacy in the Church now became the main prop of tyranny in the State. Archbishop Bancroft had been the first to teach that Diocesan or Prelatic Episcopacy was the one Apostolic and divinely-ordered mode of government, but Archbishop Laud was the first to enforce it by persecution. For him the simple duty of the Christian was to obey royal authority, and the grand business of a bishop was to enforce this. By setting the King's will above law, he became the great and revolutionary law-breaker himself. Opposition to the expressed mind of King Charles was disloyalty to the Crown! The Courts of Star Chamber and High Commission had, therefore, plenty of work, for the old Presbyterian seed was bearing a new crop. Dr. Alexander Leighton, for writing in 1630 his Presbyterian book, *Zion's Plea against the Prelacy*, was subjected to horrible mutilations and sufferings, as was also the noted lawyer William Prynne, for his many Presbyterian treatises, one of them bearing the title *Lord Bishops none of the Lord's Bishops*.

PRESBYTERIAN EXILES AND THE BRITISH SYNOD IN HOLLAND.—It is always difficult to be faithful and aggressive for Christ and yet Christianly tolerant. The first National Church to adopt and act on tolerant principles was the Presbyterian Church of Holland—a fact neither so widely known nor so frequently remembered as it should be. To Holland, therefore, the persecuted English Sectaries repaired in great numbers and found protection. But it should never be forgotten that the strongest English and Scotch churches there were Presbyterian: and that these were gathered under the exiled Presbyterian ministers into a British Synod in Holland, which Charles and Laud tried in vain for many years to bend or break. The correspondence between Laud and these ministers, which has been preserved, is exceedingly suggestive.

PRESBYTERIAN PAMPHLETS AND EARLY CHURCH DEBATES IN THE LONG PARLIAMENT, 1641.—About 30,000 pamphlets appeared in England on Church matters between 1640 and 1660. But the year 1641 must bear the palm for those on Presbyterian Church Government. We mention only three: one "written by *Smectymnuus*," an odd-looking word, made up of the initials of the five authors—S. M., Stephen Marshall; E. C., Edmund Calamy; T. Y., Thomas Young; M. N., Matthew Newcomen; and U. U. (or W.) S., William Spurston—all clergy of the Church of England. Another was by ALEXANDER HENDERSON, the great Scottish Commissioner, in which he says about Presbytery: "Here is superiority without tyranny, parity without confusion, and subjection without slavery". The last, but not least, is by JOHN MILTON, who says: "So little is it I fear lest any crookedness or wrinkle be found in Presbyterial Government . . . that every real Protestant will confess it to be the only true Church Government". Alas! Milton's high ideal was not attained by the Presbyterians, and that incensed him against them afterwards. Meanwhile, petitions in favour of the Presbyterian order were coming into Parliament, and it was evident at length that a great crisis in the Church's Government was at hand. One of the first debates in the Long Parliament was on the exclusion of Bishops from the House of Lords.

EJECTION OF BISHOPS FROM THE HOUSE OF LORDS, 1642.—The last Act passed by Charles I. before the Civil War was the bill to remove bishops from being peers. He was

driven to this very unwillingly by the dire pressure of events.
A sudden and fierce revolt had upset his own and Laud's mad
attempts to force Episcopacy on Scotland. There followed
in quick succession his *first* " Bishops' War " against Scotland ; his dismissal of the *Short* Parliament in disgust after
a brief three weeks' session, 13th April to 6th May, 1640 ;
the equally foolish and futile *second* " Bishops' War " that
same summer ; and then in November the election of the
famous *Long* Parliament, which was to last, with intervals,
for twenty years. He had to accede in 1641 to an Act of
the Scottish Parliament, which declared that "the government of the Church by bishops was repugnant to the Word
of God ". These Presbyterian triumphs told on the movement for Church reform in England. Innovations in religion, especially what was called the " et cetera " oath,*
had created immense commotion and stirred up serious
questions on the Church and its government. In the
" *Grand Remonstrance* " to the King, Parliament suggested
a special council or assembly for advising about these questions. The king's attempt to seize the five members in the
House of Commons, 4th January, 1642, and the equally
foolish action of the Bishops to retain their position and
power, made the exasperated Peers at length agree with
the Commons to pass the Bishops' Exclusion Bill. The
King signed it in February, 1642.

* The objectionable part of this oath was : " Nor will I ever give
my consent to alter the government of the Church by Archbishops,
Bishops, Deans, and Archdeacons, *et cetera*, as it stands now
established ". No one knew exactly how much the *et cetera* was
meant to include.

CHAPTER V.

Period of Presbyterian Ascendency, 1643-1649.

Parliament calls the Westminster Assembly, and both swear to the Covenant, 1643.—Three times over in 1642 did Lords and Commons pass a bill for the proposed ecclesiastical assembly. But as the King would not consent, and the war had now begun, Parliament issued its own ordinance appointing the celebrated Westminster Assembly to meet in the Abbey, 1st July, 1643. Already in January the ordinance for abolishing Episcopacy in the Church altogether had passed, and was to come into force in November. Pym and Hampden heartily agreed to this strong policy; but their early death this year was a heavy blow to the other Presbyterian leaders, such as Denzil Hollis, Glynne, Maynard, Haselrig, Sir Simonds d'Ewes, Sir Robert Harley, in the House of Commons, with the Earls of Essex, Manchester, Warwick, and Lords Brook, Fairfax, Wharton, and others among the Peers. For a time the Assembly sat in Henry VII.'s Chapel, but afterwards in the Jerusalem Chamber. The prolocutor or chairman was Dr. Twisse (and after his death Charles Herle). The assessors, or assistant chairmen, were Dr. Cornelius Burgess and John White. The clerks were Henry Roborough and

Adoniram Byfield, with Dr. John Wallis; and leading members were Edmund Calamy, Herbert Palmer, and Stephen Marshall, the foremost preacher of his day in London, Drs. John Arrowsmith, Tuckney, Lightfoot, Edward Reynolds, and Lazarus Seaman. The great event of 1643--that which committed England to Presbyterianism so far as it could be committed in a state of civil war—was the taking of THE SOLEMN LEAGUE AND COVENANT by the House of Commons and the Westminster Assembly, in St. Margaret's Church. It is most important not to confound this, as is often done, with the Scotch National Covenant of five years before. The war was going at first in favour of the King. Parliament wanted help from Scotland; and the result was the *six articles* of the Solemn League and Covenant, which was both a civil league and a religious covenant for mutual defence. It brought 20,000 Scottish troops across the border; it added six Scotch Commissioners to the Westminster Assembly, and put Presbyterianism in the ascendant.

WORK OF THE WESTMINSTER ASSEMBLY, 1643-1659.— Meanwhile the Assembly went on with its work of covenanted reformation. Its transactions may be divided into four parts:—

(1) *The Directory for Public Worship*, dealing with its three great parts of preaching, prayer, and praise, together with the sacraments, and giving directions for the conduct of each part. The Directory contains no set forms of worship as in a Liturgy, but is exactly what its name implies: a help, a guide, and a stimulus to ministers in conducting all the parts of public worship with reverence and decorum.

Its brief chapter on *Preaching* is very valuable, and contains the pith of all instructions on the subject by men who were themselves unequalled masters of this sacred art. Regarding *Prayer*, while the lawfulness of stated forms is not denied and the need for studied prayers is assumed, special anxiety is manifested that ministers should stir up this gracious devotional gift of the Holy Spirit within them; should take pains to grow in its exercise as they grow in their Christian experience; and should avoid the slovenliness of mere extemporary or unpremeditated supplications, by training themselves to deepen, vary, and enrich their devotions not less than their sermons, cultivating directness, simplicity, and warmth of address. With regard to *Praise*, the Assembly gave the preference to the Metrical Psalms of Mr. Francis Rous, one of their own number, a lay-assessor, and Member of Parliament from Cornwall, afterwards Provost of Eton; and this is substantially the so-called Scotch Version still in use.

In this Directory there is drawn out, with much care and forethought, a free and flexible method of public worship, professedly based on Scripture, which has been adopted and followed in its main features by all sections of English-speaking Protestants who do not use a Liturgical service, and yet which is not in itself incompatible with Liturgical forms. Some in the Assembly would, indeed, have preferred a reform of the old Liturgy as an alternative: but the political exigencies of the Parliament seemed to require that the Book of Common Prayer should be wholly forbidden and its place taken by the Directory mode of Worship, although many, even of those who preferred the latter, doubted the wisdom of this extreme step at that time (1645).

(2) *The Form of Presbyterial Church Government*, which occasioned such long debates with the five Dissenting brethren or Independents specially about the two points of ordination and Presbyterial discipline. Parliament voted for Presbyterianism, although much delay was occasioned even after the Assembly had sent up its Original Draft to it

in July, 1645. This *Form of Presbyterian Church Government and Ordination of Ministers* set forth: 1. "That Christ hath instituted a government and governors ecclesiastical in the Church;" that "ordination to the ministry should be by Presbyters;" and that, contrary to the idea of the Independents, "it is very requisite that no single congregation, which can conveniently associate with others, should assume to itself all and sole power of ordination;" and 2. "That for officers in a single congregation, while there ought to be one at least to labour in word and doctrine as well as rule, it is also requisite that there should be others to join with him in government".

But while these things are requisite to the *being* of a Church, there are others things requisite rather to its *well-being*. Of this latter kind are Presbyteries and Synods, with their respective powers, relations, and best methods of working.

When the Westminster Divines maintained that "Scripture doth hold forth that many particular Congregations *may* be under one Presbyterial government," and that "Synodical Assemblies *may* lawfully be of several sorts, as provincial, national, or ecumenical," they show by the permissive style they use, how clearly they discriminated between the Essentials and the non-Essentials of a scriptually constituted system of Church Government. Their theory is a very liberal and a truly Catholic one. It did not allow them to unchurch any body of professing Christians whatsoever. It enabled them to speak of Independents and others always as "brethren" in Christ's Church, even when most vehemently contending with them. For wherever they recognised Christ, there they felt bound to recognise and acknowledge the Church. Thus the distinction they made between the positive requisites or essentials of a Church, and wherein lay what was best only for a Church's interests, was, and still continues to be, one of the grand safeguards, on the part of all intelligent Presbyterians, against bigotry and narrow sectarianism.

The Assembly's Draft of its Presbyterian Directory was ready for the Parliament in July, 1645. Parliament at once brought the *ordination part* of it into use: but the full "*Form of Church-Government to be used in the Church of England and Ireland*" was not passed as an ordinance till 29th August, 1648, on account of the serious debates and misunderstanding we are now to mention.

(3) The *Erastian Controversy* as to the amount of *Autonomy* or self-governing power to be allowed within the Church. Parliament wanted the whole spiritual as well as ecclesiastical control: and it was here Parliament and Assembly quarrelled, and the fatal delay occurred in setting up full Presbyterian Government.

The two points here involved were these: whether the Lord Jesus had appointed a Government in the Church distinct from the Civil Government; and whether the power of spiritual discipline and Church-censures be by divine appointment lodged in the Church herself and her own office-bearers. Both these claims were implied in the Directory of Presbyterian Government: but Parliament resolutely set itself against them, being very jealous of all independent Church power, and being determined to keep in its own hand the full ecclesiastical *supremacy*, which in England (though not in Scotland) had belonged to the Crown or the Civil Authority.

This Parliamentary *Erastianism* (or the doctrine that there is neither spiritual independence, nor divine right of self-government in the Church) led to a series of vehement contentions between the Assembly and Parliament on these vital questions; and, although matters of difference were in some measure arranged, and Presbyterian Ordinances at length were passed, harmony and confidence were never fully restored between them.

(4) The preparation of the CONFESSION OF FAITH and the CATECHISMS. The Westminster Assembly was far, however, from being occupied with mere wrangling and debate. Much noble and permanently valuable work was done. Enduring monuments of learned and consecrated toil remain in the *Confession of Faith* and the *Larger* and *Shorter Catechisms*. Carefully drafted by some of the ablest divines, nineteen chapters of the Confession were finished by 25th September, 1646, and the remainder before the end of the year. Some of the later or disciplinary portions were not approved by Parliament for reasons already given. In April, 1647, six hundred copies of an edition with the proof-texts from Scripture were ordered to be printed by Parliament, but the document was not authoritatively issued till June, 1648.

Doctrinally, the Confession is of the moderately Calvinistic type, on which all seemed fairly well agreed. This was the prevailing type of doctrinal teaching in the English Church from the Reformation. Calvinism is, however, to many, still a bugbear, because of their grotesque misconception of it. Yet, what is it but simply the religion of the Lord's Prayer, which teaches us to pray first for God before we pray for ourselves and others: to say "Hallowed be *Thy* Name: *Thy* Kingdom come: *Thy* Will be done," before we say give *us*, forgive *us*, and the like? This is the teaching that sets God and man in their proper place and relation. In the old and false astronomy the earth was regarded as the centre of all, and took the chief place. Now, we know it is not. So in the moral universe, God is first and supreme: redemption, in all its parts, flows from his free and sovereign grace and spontaneous love: the saved have no stronger claim on God's mercy than others under condemnation, and must be ready to ascribe their salvation entirely to his unsearchable riches, giving *all* the glory to him. Whatever people may be in their professed creed, they cannot but be Calvinists in their prayers and praise, saying: "For *Thine* is the Kingdom, and the power, and the glory, for ever and ever. Amen."

THE SHORTER CATECHISM.—At least a dozen members of the Assembly had written catechisms themselves. A committee was appointed so early as 1643, which first proceeded with "The Larger Catechism," and, when that was approaching completion, a small committee was appointed, with Herbert Palmer, and after his death Dr. Tuckney, as convener, to prepare a "Shorter Catechism". But it was not till November, 1647, that the Shorter Catechism was ready for approval in Parliament, and the proofs from Scripture were not added till April, 1648. It is impossible to say who had most to do with it; but singularly enough the Scotch Commissioners had *least*, as all except Rutherford had left before it was begun. John Wallis, D.D., one of the clerks, and afterwards the famous Mathematical Professor at Oxford, may have given it the final touches. He was the first to publish an exposition or popular commentary on it, in 1657; and it is easy to count thirty others since his day. The Shorter Catechism has been translated into many languages—so early as 1656 into Latin, at Cambridge; and into both Latin and Greek by Professor Harmer, at Oxford, in 1660. Richard Baxter says: "I take it for the best catechism that I ever yet saw". Dr. Johnson thought it "one of the most sublime works of the human understanding". Dr. Philip Schaff reckons it "one of three typical catechisms of Protestantism which are likely to last to the end of time". And Thomas Carlyle wrote at the close of his life: "The older I grow—and I now stand on the brink of eternity—the more comes back to me the first sentence in the Catechism which I learned when a child, and the fuller and deeper its meaning becomes—'Man's chief end is to glorify God and to enjoy Him for ever'".

THE ASSEMBLY'S BRIEF DOCTRINAL STATEMENT.—The following brief paper of Christian Doctrine was prepared by the Assembly, and required by the Parliament to be known by all who should be admitted to the Lord's Table; the examination and judgment in each case being in the hands "of the Eldership of every Congregation".

(1) *Of one God in Three Persons.*—That there is a God: That there is but one ever-living and true God, Maker of heaven and earth and Governor of all things: That this only true God is the God whom we worship: That this God is but one, yet three distinct Persons, the Father, Son, and Holy Ghost, all equally God.

(2) *Of Man's Creation and Fall.*—That God created man after His own image, in knowledge, righteousness, and true holiness: That by one man sin entered into the world, and death by sin, and so death passed upon all men for that all have sinned: That thereby they are all dead in trespasses and sins, and are by nature the children of wrath, and so liable to eternal death, the wages of every sin.

(3) *Of Christ the Mediator.* — That there is but one Mediator between God and man, the man Christ Jesus, who is also God over all blessed for ever, neither is there salvation in any other: That He was created by the Holy Ghost and born of the Virgin Mary: That He died upon the cross to save His people from their sins: That He rose again upon the third day from the dead, ascended into heaven, sits at

the right hand of God, and makes continual intercession for us, of whose fulness we receive all grace necessary to salvation.

(4) *Of Faith, Repentance, and Holy Life.*—That Christ and His benefits are applied only by faith: That faith is the gift of God, and that we have it not of ourselves, but it is wrought in us by the Word and Spirit of God: That faith is that grace whereby we believe and trust in Christ for remission of sins and life everlasting, according to the promise of the Gospel that whosoever believes not on the Son of God shall not see life but shall perish eternally: That all they who truly repent of their sins, do see them, sorrow for them, and turn unto the Lord, and that except men repent they shall surely perish: That a godly life is conscionably ordered according to the Word of God, in holiness and righteousness, without which no man shall see God.

(5) *Of the Sacraments.*—That the Sacraments are seals of the Covenant of Grace in the Word of Christ: That the Sacraments of the New Testament are Baptism and the Lord's Supper: That the outward elements in the Lord's Supper are Bread and Wine, and do signify the Body and Blood of Christ crucified, which the worthy receiver by faith doth partake of in this Sacrament, which Christ hath likewise ordained for the remembrance of His death: That whosoever eats and drinks unworthily is guilty of the Body and Blood of the Lord, and therefore that every one is to examine himself lest he eat and drink judgment to himself, not discerning the Lord's Body.

(6) *Of the Souls and Bodies of Men after Death.*—That the souls of the faithful after death do immediately live with Christ in blessedness, and that the souls of the wicked do immediately go into hell torments: That there shall be a resurrection of the bodies both of the just and unjust at the

last day, at which time all shall appear before the Judgment Seat of Christ, according to what they have done in the body, whether it be good or evil: And that the righteous shall go into life eternal and the wicked into everlasting punishment.

CLOSE OF THE ASSEMBLY.—The Westminster Assembly sat till 22nd February, 1649, a little over five years and a half, holding 1163 sessions. It then was continued as a committee for trial and licence of ministers till Cromwell broke up the Long Parliament, 25th March, 1652, when it dispersed without any formal dissolution. The seal adopted by the Assembly was an open Bible surrounded with palm leaves: this was introduced in 1876 into the emblem of the Presbyterian Church of England. No body of divines, perhaps, has ever been more recklessly and vigorously abused than the Westminster Assembly. All modern and intelligent opinion, however, is steadily veering round to the view so long ago expressed by good Richard Baxter: "The divines there congregated were men of eminent learning and godliness, and ministerial abilities and fidelity: and, being not worthy to be one of them myself, I may the more freely speak that truth which I know, even in the face of malice and envy, that, as far as I am able to judge by the information of all history of that kind and by any other evidences left us, the Christian world, since the days of the Apostles, had never a Synod of more excellent divines (taking one thing with another) than this Synod and the Synod of Dort were".

PRESBYTERIAN LONDON, 1643-1649.—To speak of Presbyterian London may sound strange to modern ears. Yet this is exactly what London did become under the Long Parliament. For after the adoption of the Solemn League and Covenant in September, 1643, London grew more and more Presbyterian in its sympathies, although Presbyterian worship and order did not come into full operation over the city and suburbs till August, 1646. The long delay arose from the protracted debates in the Westminster Assembly on points of Church government, but particularly from the serious misunderstanding between Assembly and Parliament as to complete spiritual independence, or the amount of self-governing power to be allowed to the Church. Parliament wished those who might come under Church discipline to have a right of appeal to a *civil* tribunal. Against this both the Assembly and the London ministers strongly protested, and although with difficulty the matter was at length arranged it was not with much satisfaction to either party. The most violent feelings and the most fatal misunderstandings, however, gathered round the question whether *any* dissent or *how much* should be allowed *outside* the proposed new National Church. Swarms of religious sects had sprung up amid the convulsions of the times. TOLERATION for *orthodox* Christian sects *outside* was the watchword of the Independents. ACCOMMODATION for tender Christian consciences *inside* the Church's pale was the Presbyterian idea; for, it was said, if there is to be a *National* Church at all, must not the whole nation conform to its discipline, so far as it is truly Scriptural? Otherwise, how can it be a really *National* Church? At this very crisis the King fled to the Scottish Presbyterian army. Keen national feelings and susceptibilities were aroused. To these Milton gave strong expression, embittering English feeling against everything Scotch, and accusing the Presbyterians at the same time (more passionately than fairly) of being the grand "forcers of conscience". Meanwhile, during July and August, 1646, in spite of much opposition, TWELVE PRESBYTERIES were set up in London, including 139 parishes, within a compass of ten miles, and the FIRST

PROVINCIAL SYNOD of London met on Monday, 3rd May, 1647, in the Convocation House of St. Paul's, but always afterwards in the far-famed SION COLLEGE, where its records are still preserved. It produced some able Presbyterian books, such as *The Divine Right of the Gospel Ministry*, with a valuable *Appendix* in defence of Presbyterial Ordination.

PRESBYTERIAN CHURCH ESTABLISHED IN LANCASHIRE, 1646.—In many respects Lancashire was a remarkable county. At first the Reformation had great difficulty in getting a foothold, and Queen Elizabeth had to allow the "Prophesyings," and similar Presbyterian methods in the Manchester Collegiate Church. Nowhere in England was the struggle keener between Papist, Prelatist, and Puritan. The Civil War also first broke out in Lancashire, and it was peculiarly a *religious* struggle there. Lancashire Puritans and Scotch patriots drew, therefore, warmly together: in no other English county was the Solemn League and Covenant so largely and influentially signed. Two eminent ministers, HEYRICK, Warden of Manchester, and HERLE, Rector of Winwick, the richest living in the North, represented the county in the Westminster Assembly. In response to a huge petition, Parliament, on 2nd October, 1646, ordained the PRESBYTERIAN government and discipline to be established throughout Lancashire, with sixty parishes in NINE PRESBYTERIES, and with a PROVINCIAL SYNOD OR ASSEMBLY, which met at Preston, in May, 1649. The minutes of two of the Presbyteries still exist, and have been recently published.

PRESBYTERIANISM IN OTHER COUNTIES.—On 29th January, 1648, the ordinance of Parliament was issued "for the speedy dividing and settling the several Counties of this Kingdom into Classical Presbyteries and Congregational Elderships". And on 29th August, 1648, was issued *The Form of Church Government* for England and Ireland. The Committee of Lords and Commons drew up a list of ministers and elders for fourteen Presbyteries in Essex, and the same number in Suffolk, but owing to the uprising of the army against Parliament these arrangements never took full effect. In Cheshire, again (where, from the days of Christopher Goodman and William Whittingham to those of Matthew Henry, many Presbyterian names occur such as John Ley, John Paget, and Adam Martindale), the Presbyterian petition from fifty-nine ministers remained a dead letter, and the movement was suddenly checked, as in other counties and for the same reason.

ENGLISH PRESBYTERIANS AND THEIR WORK IN AMERICA. —Meanwhile Puritanism of the Presbyterian type had gone forth with the first English emigrants to Virginia and other American colonies, although Presbyterian Huguenots of France were the earliest of all refugees to the American shores. The grand heroes of the little ship MAYFLOWER, in 1620, were of the Independent persuasion, but those of 1625 and of 1629 were Presbyterians, whose charter contained a memorable missionary purpose to "win and incite the natives of the country to the knowledge and obedience of the only true God and Saviour of mankind, and the Christian faith". Of the 22,000 emigrants who had gone to New England before 1640 not fewer than 4000 were Presbyterians. The Presbyterian views of JOHN ELIOT, the apostle to the Indians, and the connection between his missionary work and the Presbyterians of England, are specially notable. For a missionary society was started by an ordinance of the Long Parliament in 1649, to "propagate the Gospel in New England". Presbyterians and Independents worked harmoniously together on "the Cambridge platform" of 1648, and the later one of "Saybrook". The former provided for the Presbyterian organisation of individual congregations, with a district advisory council, while the latter advanced towards a fully-organised Presbyterianism. But it was the persecuted Presbyterian ministers, who had to flee from England after 1662, that helped, along with others from Scotland and Ireland, to lay the foundation of American Presbyterianism, which now flourishes on so vast a scale.

PART II.

DECLINE OF THE PRESBYTERIANS IN ENGLAND.

CHAPTER I.

PERIOD OF DISAPPOINTMENT AND FAILURE, 1649-1662.

HOW THE PRESBYTERIANS FAILED TO ESTABLISH THEMSELVES.—Although the Presbyterians rose to prominence and power, their time of triumph was short. Why was this? Many have thought it was because of their religious intolerance, as if they were worse than others in this respect. It was not so, neither nation nor Parliament was one whit more tolerant than they. It was not their intolerance, but the unpopular form it took, which led to their failure: they wanted all the people to be in one National Church, and tried to secure ecclesiastical unity throughout the whole of the three kingdoms. They were aiming at far too much, and wasted time in debating, instead of acting with promptitude and decision, as the circumstances required. But what raised against them the ire both of sectaries and worldly politicians was their vehement assertion of the Church's right to govern herself and exercise spiritual discipline over her members. Thus Presbyterianism was never allowed time nor opportunity to root itself in England. Its growth was too rapid and sudden, while the soil was not sufficiently prepared for its purpose; its branches were wider than its roots, and the first adverse gust blew it over. When, therefore, the Earl of Manchester and his Presbyterian supporters were driven from power by the army, in 1648, the whole constitutional reforming movement came to an end, and the revolutionary or military method took its place. The Presbyterians in London and Lancashire grew lukewarm and dubious about their position, and about the ideal Church at which they had aimed. Moreover, they could not get a sufficient number of the right kind of men to act as ruling elders. Their Church discipline was hampered and weakened by Erastian interferences and sectarian intrusions; Church property was managed by "sequestrators". The whole Presbyterian scheme was obnoxious to the army and its leaders. These were the reasons why the Presbyterians failed to hold their ascendency.

CHARGE OF INTOLERANCE ALLEGED AGAINST THEM.— This may be divided into three parts: (1) Parliament, it is said, under Presbyterian pressure passed a harsh and cruel decree, 2nd May, 1648, against all who should be found guilty of heresy or blasphemy. It is enough to reply that, severe as was this enactment, it was not a tightening but a relaxing of the law previously in force. No persecution nor martyrdom arose out of it; and, however intolerant the Presbyterians were, they were yet far more free from bigotry and persecuting practices than either Prelatists or Independents were in *their* day of power. (2) The Presbyterians, it is said, wrote against religious toleration. A famous tract of the Lancashire ministers is often quoted in support of this. But it is only fair to quote also the official *Vindication of the Presbyterial Government and Ministry*, by the London Provincial Assembly in 1649. "We abhor," they say, "an over-rigid urging of uniformity." They maintain also that it is "the duty of all Christians to hold communion together as one Church in what they agree, and mutually to tolerate and bear with one another in lesser differences". To the Presbyterians also belongs the honour of stating and upholding the fundamental principle of all true religious liberty: "*God alone is Lord of the conscience, and hath left it free from the doctrines and commandments of men, which are in anything contrary to His Word; or beside it if matters of faith or worship*". (3) It is charged that the Presbyterian ecclesiastical courts wished to exercise a tyrannical civil jurisdiction and control. What they wished was the right of "*the keys*" for themselves; the right, in other words, of the Church, apart from legal enactments or civil control, to determine who should be her members and office-bearers. This was one main cause of the rupture between Assembly and Parliament, and it was because of this Parliamentary *Erastianism* (the doctrine that there is no government in the Church apart from the civil one) that the Presbyterian Establishment was finally wrecked.

CHRISTOPHER LOVE, AN ENGLISH PRESBYTERIAN COVENANTER AND MARTYR.—The execution of Charles I., in January, 1649, was bitterly resented by the Presbyterians. As constitutional reformers, they were opposed on principle to such a step. The Scottish Parliament proclaimed Charles II. as king, and a war ensued between England and Scotland. The Presbyterians in Lancashire and London also plotted against Cromwell's military republicanism. A pious and eminent Presbyterian minister in London, Christopher Love, was charged with high treason for so doing. He was condemned to be executed, though declaring his innocence. After some hesitation and delay (during which his noble wife, Mary Love, exerted herself to save his life—the touching letters that passed between them, and her petitions to Parliament, being preserved in a famous pamphlet, called *Love's Name Lives*, 1651), the "Rump" Parliament sent him to the scaffold, on Tower Hill. He made a noble speech, avowing his readiness to die for the Covenant and for his Presbyterian principles. This shook the power of the new Commonwealth. "Most ministers and good people," says Baxter, "did look at the Commonwealth as a tyranny, and were more alienated than ever." He adds: "The soldiers said I was so like to Love myself that I should not be right till I was shorter by the head".

THE PRESBYTERIANS UNDER THE COMMONWEALTH AND PROTECTORATE. — Only in name and very partially did Presbyterian order and worship continue to have State sanction and countenance. The Solemn League and Covenant was supplanted by THE ENGAGEMENT, which ran thus: "I do promise to be true and faithful to the Commonwealth, as now established without a King or House of Lords". This had to be taken by all over eighteen years of age, and publicly by every minister, within six months. There was no persecution, but religious toleration was of a very mixed kind, and Church affairs were controlled and regulated by military lieutenants. Richard Baxter, with his large-minded views as a Presbyterian churchman, and his earnest desires as an evangelical minister, being above all anxious to bring the Gospel home to the people with quickening power, drew up his famous scheme of "*Agreement for Church Order and Concord*". He got a number of Episcopal, Presbyterian, and Independent ministers, with godly representative laymen from their Churches, to work together in monthly and quarterly parochial meetings for Gospel purposes. The principles of this notable Worcester "ASSOCIATION" were adopted and acted upon in several other counties, as in Westmoreland and elsewhere, Presbyterian ministers being the chief promoters.

RICHARD BAXTER AND HIS PECULIAR INFLUENCE.—This extraordinary man, of whom Bishop Wilkins declared that "if he had lived in the primitive time, he would have been one of the Fathers of the Church," and Dr. Isaac Barrow said "his practical writings were never mended and his controversial ones seldom confuted," was born at Rowton, Shropshire, in 1615, and played a remarkable part from the time he became minister at Kidderminster in 1641 till his death in 1691, at what must seem, from his many bodily diseases and ailments, the advanced age of 76. He was one of the most powerful and popular preachers of his day. Amid his many other exhausting labours, he wrote the almost incredible number of 168 separate books, some of them, like his *Christian Directory* or his *Catholic Theology*, enough for an ordinary man's whole life-work. How valuable, too, is his autobiography or *The Narrative of his Life and Times!* and what reader has not felt solemnised by his *Call to the Unconverted*, or charmed by his sacred classic, *The Saints' Everlasting Rest?* He early rejected Episcopacy in its English form, though willing for peace sake to adopt some modification of it, and remained a Presbyterian minister to the end without exclusiveness, and desiring to subordinate Church government and other kindred questions to the higher requirements of practical Christianity. Few have exercised a stronger influence on English Nonconformity; but his influence was not always wisely exerted. Intensely jealous for the interests of personal religion and vital godliness among men, he often thwarted his own objects by a metaphysical and speculative temper, more fitted to open the flood-gates of theological discussion than settle difficult points of doctrine, or to rouse a self-assertive antagonism rather than the spirit of Christian brotherhood which he loved. Thus, when invited by Cromwell at the close of the civil wars to assist in settling "the fundamentals of religion," on its being objected to what he proposed, that "it might be subscribed by a Papist or Socinian," he replied: "So much the better and so much the fitter it is to be the matter of concord". His hatred to, and his suffering under, the penally enforced imposition of the entire Prayer Book and the whole of the 39 Articles, led him into many unguarded utterances, so that when the dangerous outcry arose next century against definite creeds or doctrinal subscription, which wrought such havoc among the Presbyterians, many were ready to quote good Richard Baxter as lending them support, who never shared his holy, devoted, and evangelical spirit.

PRESBYTERIANISM IN THE BALANCE.—When Cromwell died—on that tempestuous night, 3rd September, 1658, which was the anniversary of his great victories, Dunbar and Worcester—the Commonwealth began to fall to pieces. His unambitious son Richard succeeded him, but could not cope with the military factions of Lambert and Fleetwood. His sympathies were with the Presbyterians. General Monk also, bringing up his troops from Scotland, and declaring against the "Rump" and in favour of the Long Parliament with the Presbyterian members in their places again, told the assembled Commons that "moderate Presbyterian government appeared the true way to the Church's settlement". And so it came about that, at the time when by Monk's cunning arrangement Charles II. was restored, 29th May, 1660, the Presbyterians were once more the Established Church, with, however, express toleration for tender consciences—an arrangement for which these Presbyterians do not always get credit. To save the country on the brink of ruin, and to prevent it falling a prey to military adventurers, they had heartily promoted the King's return, his Royal *Declaration from Breda* having allayed all their fears. But how miserably repaid was their self-sacrificing loyalty! Milton's warning words, in his *Defence of the People of England*, were soon to come true: "Woe be to you Presbyterians especially, if ever any of Charles's race recover the sceptre! Believe me, *you* shall pay all the reckoning!"

CHAPTER II.

The Heroic Period, 1662-1688.

Act of Uniformity and Ejection of the Two Thousand, 1662.—For a time the King and his advisers seemed conciliatory to the Presbyterians, who had done so much for the Restoration, offering Calamy, Baxter and others bishoprics, deaneries, and similar honours. But the pretence did not last long, for it was seen that the weary and exhausted nation would accept any ecclesiastical settlement the Court might propose. The Presbyterians were divided in counsel. A small section, led by Drs. Lazarus Seaman and William Jenkyn, would have no compromise; but the great body, with Calamy, Baxter, and Manton, were willing to accept a modified Episcopacy, if they were left free to hold their essential principles. The hypocritical steps by which these Presbyterians were first deceived, then betrayed, and finally ejected, will always be painful to the honest mind. Sir Edward Hyde (Lord Clarendon) and Sheldon, who became Bishop of London, and afterwards Archbishop of Canterbury, are chiefly responsible. The *Declaration of Breda* was violated. Certain proposals and concessions made to the Presbyterians in the *Worcester House Declaration* were hypocritical; and the *Savoy Conference* between the Bishops' party and the Presbyterians was a mere pretence to save appearances. The *Pension* Parliament (which got that name from so many of its members being in the pay of Charles II. and Louis XIV. of France) decreed to burn the Solemn League and Covenant, to restore the Bishops and their jurisdiction, and to pass the "Corporation or Test Act"—an act of vengeance. A great reaction was setting in. The Court party took full advantage of this to crush and humiliate the Presbyterians by the all-important *Act of Uniformity*. The interval between 19th May, when it was passed, and 24th August, when it should come into force, was one of deep anxiety to the Presbyterian ministers. They could heartily take the oath of allegiance, but they could not comply with the other three principal conditions —that they should be Episcopally re-ordained, give their unfeigned assent and consent to *everything* in the Prayer Book, and take an oath to abjure the Covenant. Rather than violate their consciences, two thousand ministers, most of them Presbyterian, gave up their churches, parsonages, and livings, casting themselves and their families on the providence of God. Among these were such distinguished men as Richard Baxter, the elder Calamy, Dr. William Bates, John Howe, Dr. Manton, John Flavel, Matthew Poole, Philip Henry, and many others of like worth.

THEIR SUFFERINGS AND PERSECUTION.—Such books as Heylin's virulent *History of the Presbyterians* and the amusing but rancorous burlesque of *Hudibras* were eagerly licensed by the Court at this juncture, and did more, perhaps, than all others to poison the springs of truth, and to prejudice English nature against the noble army of the ejected and their fallen cause. No provision was made to save them from starvation. The Long Parliament had in its day more mercifully secured a fifth of each living for the clergy it ejected. But now, by fixing St. Bartholomew's Day for the ejection, the ministers were even cheated out of a quarter's stipend, for which they had worked! It was as pitifully mean as it was cruel and unjust. Many of the sufferers endured terrible hardships, and their pathetic story has been preserved in Baxter's *Own Life and Times*, and especially in Dr. Edmund Calamy's *Account of the Ejected*, where their names and memories are embalmed for all time to come. Yet the Government remained fiercely implacable; and in the spirit of Sheldon, who said: "If we had thought so many of the Presbyterian clergy had conformed we would have made the door even straiter," they proceeded to pass the terrible Clarendon Code of persecuting statutes against them; the *Conventicle Act*, which broke up the little attached flocks that clung to their ejected pastors; the *Five Mile Act*, which drove them into rural exile; and the *Oxford Act*, which deprived them of university and other education, and committed so many to prison. Only little gleams of favour visited them occasionally, as in THE INDULGENCE of 1672, when certain preaching licences were issued in favour of particularly designated persons or places. But even these were soon stopped.

THE LOWEST DEPTH.—Things were at their worst in 1684, the last year of Charles II.'s reign, and this continued during the reign of his brother, James II. Just as the darkest hour is before the dawn, the blackest time was 1684-1688, immediately before the Revolution. Never had public spirit fallen so low, nor the national temper been so abject. The very climate was at its worst in 1684. It was a winter of the most awful frost, and a summer of the most awful drought. Every sacred interest of patriotism, piety, and principle was blighted too. The Divine right of kings alone was flourishing; their Divine right to do wrong and command others to do so was fashionable doctrine with the Anglican clergy. Charles had secured the succession to the throne for his Popish brother, and seemed almost within reach of despotic power; happily for the country, this was prevented by his frivolous character, his spendthrift habits, and his tricky policy. The prisons were crowded with venerable ministers; the courts of justice were thronged with base informers, who were ready for money to swear anything against them; and the best of men suffered maltreatment, and were even brought to the scaffold for their religion's sake. But James II.'s Popish bigotry and stubborn folly soon ended his own reign and the twenty-eight years' persecution together!

PHILIP HENRY.—This ejected Presbyterian minister never thought of fame; but his charming character and the beauty of his holiness are embalmed for us in Matthew Henry's Life of his Father, the family Memoirs edited by Sir J. B. Williams, and his own Diaries.

His Childhood.—Philip Henry was born 24th August, 1631, within the grounds of Whitehall Palace, his father, a Welshman, being keeper of the postern or garden gate admitting Privy Councillors and others who came by the river. "The witnesses at my baptism were Philip, Earl of Pembroke, who gave me his Christian name and was kind to me till his death; James, Earl of Carlisle; and the Countess of Salisbury." Philip Henry did no discredit to such a birthplace and such sponsors. He grew up a well-favoured child, with a graceful suavity which never left him. The young princes were his occasional associates, Prince Charles, afterwards Charles II., being a year older, and Prince James, afterwards James II., two years younger. His pious Puritan mother trained him and his sisters with the utmost care. The Long Parliament and its great events he knew, being a child of ten at the time of the king's rash attempt to seize its patriot leaders. Philip Henry was to choose the Presbyterian side in the coming struggle, both as a constitutional loyalist and as a Puritan Churchman. But he cherished grateful memories of the royal family and of Archbishop Laud himself, whom he saw last in the Tower, and from whom he received some newly-coined money.

At Westminster School and Christ Church College, Oxford.—Philip Henry was a fine instance of Christian boyhood. Admitted at the age of twelve to Westminster School, he became a favourite pupil with its famous head master, Dr. Busby, and assisted him with his Greek Grammar. He lost his mother in 1645, but writing two years after, at the age of sixteen, he could say: "The Lord was now graciously pleased to bring me home effectually to Himself". He became a distinguished student of Christ Church, Oxford, and got his degree of Master of Arts in December, 1652.

Ordained Minister of Worthenbury.—His heart had been long set on being a preacher of the Gospel. This led him to spend all the rest of his life in that bit of Flintshire which is so curiously cut off from the rest, and enclosed by Shropshire, Denbigh, and Cheshire. Lady Puleston, of Emral Hall, besought him to come here to teach her sons, and preach in the neighbourhood. Like her, he was now firmly attached to the Presbyterian party. He had seen its order and worship come fully into operation in London about 1646, and his keen schoolboy intelligence had been deeply affected and interested. So he writes, under 6th July, 1657: "I made addresses to the Presbytery of Shropshire for ordination". Lady Puleston had told him: "You have done more good these six months than I have seen these eighteen years". Thus at the age of twenty-six he was admitted to Worthenbury, the newly-endowed parish of the Pulestons, saying solemnly : " Lord, I seek not theirs, but them ; give me the souls, let whoso will take the goods. Oh, that God would add seals to my ministry ! "

The Ejected Presbyterian at Broad Oak.—In 1660 Philip Henry secured as his wife Katherine Matthews, only child and heiress of one of the older families in the district. But trying times were now at hand. For though Philip Henry favoured and promoted the Restoration, he had bitter experience of the changes it wrought. Judge and Lady Puleston were now dead ; and the young squire, imbibing the low tastes that began to prevail, gave him much trouble. He watched with pain and surprise the vindictive measures of the "Pension" Parliament; and on the passing of the Act of Uniformity he said : "I would rather lose my all and save my conscience". St. Bartholomew's Day found him, therefore, among the ejected ; he called the 24th of August " the day I was born in 1631, and the day I died by law in 1662, as did also near 2000 other faithful ministers of Jesus Christ". Happily his wife's marriage portion, the sweet little farm of Broad Oak, was ready for them ; a few weeks later Matthew was born. Here he was able to give help and hospitality to his poorer and less fortunate brethren. Philip Henry is the family saint of those days. Broad Oak became a proverb for all that was best in a happy and well-ordered home. During the twenty-eight sad years of persecution he often suffered heavy fines and imprisonment for conscience sake. He preserved, however, a large-hearted Christian charity, and was no narrow schismatic. But he did stand fast to THE COVENANT, maintaining "that, though particular instruments might miscarry, it was in general the cause of God and religion, as will in due time be made to appear". At the Revolution, in 1688, he benefited by its liberty and toleration; he became more abundant in labours and was greatly revered by all his brethren. He survived till 1696.

PRESBYTERIAN PURITANISM—ITS REAL NATURE AND VITALITY.—The fall of Puritanism, though severe, was only temporary. Such cases as Philip Henry and other like-minded heroes of the ejectment showed that their cause had too much vital principle in it to be wholly extinguished, however long and painfully it might suffer eclipse. As a leading modern historian (Green) has said: "It was from the moment of its seeming fall its victory began. . . . In the Revolution of 1688 Puritanism did the work of civil liberty, which it had failed to do in 1642. It wrought out, through Wesley and the revival of the 18th century, the work of religious reform. . . . The history of English progress since the Restoration, on its moral and spiritual sides, has been the history of Puritanism." To the great mass of the old Puritans or Nonconformists *inside the Church* the Presbyterial order of things was dear as a Scriptural Institution and as a sound method of Church reform. But it was only a means to an end. They were not contending merely for a form of Church Government for its own sake. Their main purpose had ever been to get the Church freed from superstitious usages and mediæval corruptions; to secure an active *preaching* clergy as distinct from mere service-mumblers; and to have the Word of God made a living reality in the hearts and homes of the people. A few extracts from *The Character of the Old English Puritan or Church Nonconformist*, by one of themselves, may set this matter in its proper light. "The old English Puritan was one that honoured God above all, and under God would give everyone his due, making the Word of God the grand rule. He highly esteemed order in the house of God, but would not, under colour of that, submit to superstitious rites. He reverenced authority keeping within its sphere, but durst not, under pretext of subjection to the higher powers, worship God after the traditions of men. He thought God had left a rule in His Word for Church discipline, and that aristocratical by elders, not monarchical by bishops, nor democratical by the people. Right discipline, however, he judged as pertaining not to the being but to the well-being of a Church; therefore, he esteemed those Churches most pure where government is by elders, yet he unchurched not those where it was otherwise. He endeavoured to have the scandalous cast out of Communion; bewailing corruptions and seeking to amend them, without, however, separating himself where he might partake in the worship and not in the corruption. He put not holiness in Church-buildings, and would have them decent, not magnificent. His chiefest music was singing of Psalms, wherein, though he neglected not the melody of the voice, he looked chiefly after that of the heart. He was much in prayer, public and private, esteeming that manner of prayer best where, by the gift of God, expressions were varied according to present wants and occasions. Yet he did not account set forms unlawful, nor wholly reject the Liturgy, but the corruptions of it. He accounted preaching as necessary now as in the primitive Church, and esteemed that preaching best wherein was most of God and least of man. The Lord's Day he was careful to improve as a divine ordinance: yet he knew the liberty God gave for needful refreshing. The family he endeavoured to make a Church, labouring, that those born into it might be born again unto God. His whole life he accounted a warfare: Christ his captain, the Cross his banner, and his watchward 'he who suffers, conquers'." Thus, as another leading English historian (Prof. Gardiner) has said: "The distinctive feature of Puritanism was . . . its clear conception of the immediate relation between every individual soul of God, and that every man was intrusted with a work for the benefit of his fellow-creatures. . . . Under these watchwords of faith and duty our English liberties were won; and, however much the outward forms of Puritanism may have fallen into decay, it is certain that, under the same watchwords alone, they will be preserved as a heritage to our children." Puritanism, even Presbyterian Puritanism with all its faults and failings, has, therefore, a great and glorious future before it, as well as a great and glorious past behind it.

CHAPTER III.

Toleration and Meeting-House Building Period, 1688-1710.

Toleration or Comprehension?—A new era opened for the Presbyterians in England, Scotland, and Ireland at the Revolution of 1688. The arrival of WILLIAM OF ORANGE delivered the Protestant interest from its state of peril. But, with his more liberal Dutch Presbyterian notions, he considered what Parliament proposed in the TOLERATION ACT as too small a measure of religious liberty. He wished room to be made in the Church of England for Presbyterians and other Nonconformists. The famous "Comprehension Bill" was therefore brought into the House of Lords, so as "to unite their Majesties' Protestant subjects". With this view a Commission was appointed, which suggested an immense number of changes in the Prayer Book and Statutes, such as the Presbyterians had always desired. But the Church and Clergy were not ready for so sweeping a reform, and this last attempt at "Comprehension" failed. The Presbyterians had to be content, therefore, with the Toleration Act, which secured for them, along with others, liberty of publicly worshipping in their own way. But the law did not sanction the setting up of Presbyteries and Synods, and the oppressive *Test* and *Corporation* Acts still remained. These acts deprived all Nonconformists of civil offices and privileges except under conditions which their consciences could not endure.

THE CELEBRATED "ENQUIRY," 1691.—A notable book, in favour of Presbyterians being comprehended in the National Church, was written at this time, with the title: "An Enquiry into the Constitution, Discipline, Unity, and Worship of the Primitive Church that flourished within the first 300 years after Christ". Its design was to show how Presbyterian the Primitive Church was, and to plead for union and conciliation on this ground. The book made a great sensation, and called forth several replies. The author, Peter King, did not give his name; he was a young Presbyterian layman, nephew of John Locke, who afterwards studied law, and rose at last to be Lord High Chancellor of Great Britain, dying in 1734 at the age of sixty-five. It was this book which afterwards made John Wesley a Presbyterian in Church theory and practice.

THE EARLY PRESBYTERIAN MEETING-HOUSES.—By the Revolution the Church of Scotland was restored to its Presbyterian order. In England, however, the Presbyterians were Nonconformists, and formed the leading part of "the Dissenting interest". They had to build places of worship for themselves and maintain Christian ordinances out of their own pockets. The last ten years of the seventeenth century and the first ten years of the eighteenth may be called the meeting-house building era. England had never seen anything like it before. In a single generation about a thousand of such *meeting-houses* (for that was their name then, and not churches or chapels) sprang up, at great cost and self-sacrifice; and the great bulk of them especially the larger ones, were Presbyterian. Their chief feature was the high-pitched hip-roof, with curved pantiles, whence their attenders were, in some localities, nick-named "Pantilers". The schism that rent the Church of England gave safety and security for a time to Dissent. Archbishop Sancroft, with Ken and other bishops, and four hundred Clergy, refused the oath of allegiance to William and Mary, and formed the separate Church of the Nonjurors. This lowered the power and credit of Anglicanism, and led to bitter internal divisions and controversies.

PECULIARITIES OF THE NEW PRESBYTERIAN POSITION.— According to Dr. Calamy, the bulk of the Presbyterians in England would have liked a Church government "as it is legally established in North Britain". The Toleration Act, however, gave protection only to separate worshipping assemblies which declared their loyal attachment to the *doctrinal*, as distinct from the episcopal and ceremonial section of the Thirty-nine Articles; but it did not permit the working of the feared and hated Presbyterian system itself. Presbyterian "meetings" were narrowly watched, and had all to be registered in the Episcopal Courts or at Quarter Sessions. They looked like Independent Churches, but two things distinguished them from the Independents. (1) They had no "Church meetings," so that Church-members did not rule; but the whole responsibility of admitting to Church privileges and of administering discipline rested with the minister. (2) They attached great importance to ordination by Presbyters, which they thought should be an ordination to the work and office of the Holy Ministry, and not to a mere pastoral relationship to any particular Church or congregation. They were fond of ministerial "associations," which were created for this and other purposes; and these many of them called "Presbyteries". Until the Revolution these ordinations had been all conducted secretly, the first one being at Manchester, 1672. The first public one was in Yorkshire in 1689, when five young ministers were ordained, but the first to attract public attention was that of Calamy and six others, in 1694, in London.

"HAPPY UNION" OF PRESBYTERIANS AND INDEPENDENTS, 1690-1694.—Feeling they had great ends and interests in common, the Presbyterian and Independent ministers of London drew up their famous " Heads of Agreement," to promote co-operation in their work, and to prevent collisions. Both parties made concessions; but the Presbyterians yielded most by surrendering the Presbyterial jurisdiction over congregations and ministers, reserving only a right of appeal to occasional Synodical gatherings. The Independents, however, made great approaches toward Presbyterianism in consenting to fixed ministerial associations for mutual advice as well as for ordination; in ordaining men to the office of the holy ministry, apart from any specific pastoral charge; and in allowing that "it belongs to the pastors and elders to rule and govern" in the Church, and " the brotherhood to *consent*, according to the rule of the Gospel ".

The united ministers formed a joint FUND under a Central Board, to aid weak Churches, train students for the ministry, and supply the Gospel in necessitous districts. Provincial ASSOCIATIONS, or CLASSES, as they were often called, sprang up over the country on a basis similar to that of the London Union, among the most famous being those of *Exeter and Devonshire*, where the godly JOHN FLAVEL was the first Moderator, *Lancashire*, and *Cheshire*, which was promoted by MATTHEW HENRY, *Cumberland* and *Westmoreland*, and *Northumberland*, where Dr. RICHARD GILPIN was the leading spirit. Dr. Gilpin, who had been Rector of Greystoke, and who, like his illustrious relative Bernard Gilpin before him, had declined the Bishopric of Carlisle, became the first Presbyterian minister in Newcastle-on-Tyne.

RUPTURE OF THE UNION IN LONDON. DR. DANIEL WILLIAMS AND THE ANTINOMIAN CONTROVERSY.—The "Associations" had a tendency to develop in a Presbyterian direction; and this caused great uneasiness among the Independent ministers in London. What, however, broke up the "Union" was the violent theological controversy which raged like a kind of frenzy around the honoured name of Dr. Daniel Williams from 1692 to 1699. He was one of the most eminent and influential ministers of his day in London; a strong and pronounced Presbyterian in his views; very wealthy and benevolent; founder of the now famous WILLIAMS' LIBRARY and in many other ways a princely giver for the Gospel to succeeding ages. The *Memoirs of his Life and Eminent Conduct* were written by his warm friend and admirer, Daniel Defoe. Many of the well-meaning but less instructed among the Dissenting ministers began to preach about Christ's death and His satisfaction for His people's sins, as though Christians had little or nothing to do with the Divine law. So they spoke of the Gospel as if it were all privilege and little or no responsibility, and they made the doctrines of grace weaken rather than strengthen the sense of Christian duty and obligation. Dr. Williams was invited by his Presbyterian brethren to write against this abuse. His enemies charged him with going to the opposite extreme, and they tried hard to blacken his character. A bitter controversy ensued, which did great damage to the "Dissenting Interest," and was the first thing to rob its pulpits of warm and genial evangelical unction and of the old converting power.

MATTHEW HENRY, THE CELEBRATED COMMENTATOR, now comes to the front as a Presbyterian minister, the worthy son of his no less worthy father, Philip Henry.

His Early Life.—Matthew Henry was born at Broad Oak, in the township of Iscoed, Flintshire, 18th October, 1662. This was the year of " Black Bartholomew," and he ever esteemed it an honour and responsibility to be a child of the ejectment. Carefully and piously trained with his four sisters in their happy home, he was sent at the age of seventeen to be under a somewhat remarkable man, the Rev. Thomas Doolittle, M.A., the courageous founder of the *very first meeting-house* in London, who was to be the *last survivor* of his ejected brethren there, and who was now the first to venture also on opening an institution for training a Presbyterian ministry outside the National Church. When the persecuting authorities broke this up and scattered the twenty-eight students, Matthew Henry entered himself as a law student at Gray's Inn, but privately pursued his divinity course. He was secretly ordained in London, 9th May, 1687, being, like his father, a thorough Presbyterian Puritan, and, like him also, having a warmly evangelical and catholic spirit.

His Presbyterial Position and Ministry.—At the age of twenty-five Matthew Henry was settled in Chester, with which town his name and labours must always remain associated. He ministered here over twenty-five years, and only two years before his death he removed to Hackney, London. He took great interest in the Cheshire "Association" of ministers, which he calls a "Presbytery," and of which he was secretary, its minutes being still in existence. A new "meeting-house" was built for him in 1700. Amid his earnest and varied labours he wrote much, his father's *Life* being a very precious biography. His great work was his still popular COMMENTARY, which, however, he did not live to finish, the *sixth* volume, from *Romans* to *Revelation*, being completed by friends after his death. He struggled hard against the evil times in which he lived, and toiled bravely and faithfully for his Master amidst many difficulties. He died suddenly 22nd June, 1714, at the age of fifty-one, after a fall from his horse at Nantwich, where he had preached his *first* sermon, and where also he preached his *last*.

CHAPTER IV.

Transitional and Spasmodic Period, 1710-1740.

Trying and Changing Influences at Work, from 1710.—For twenty years after the Revolution of 1688 the Presbyterians continued in a flourishing and highly-promising condition, with wealthy merchants and landed proprietors in their ranks, and not a few prominent representatives in town and city corporations. Subtle and deadly changes, however, were now at work. The Universities had been closed since 1662 to all except members of the Church of England, and this proved a cunning and disastrous blow to Presbyterian progress. When the grand old veteran band of ejected and suffering ministers died out, their less educated and less distinguished successors could hardly fill their place. Some, too, of the ablest young Presbyterian students who sought University training fell back into the National Church, such as the afterwards celebrated Bishop Butler and his friend and fellow-student Secker, who rose to be Archbishop of Canterbury. Virulent political feeling also ran high, and this was hurtful, especially when the bigoted High-Church reaction set in under Queen Anne in 1710. By the Union of 1707 Scottish Presbyterians were admitted to the

Parliament at Westminster. On this and other accounts the furious cry arose: "The Church in danger; down with Dissenters!" and the "Sacheverell" mobs destroyed many meeting-houses. Two disgraceful Acts of Parliament followed in 1713—the *Schism Bill*, designed to stop all Dissenting teachers and teaching whatsoever; and the Bill *against occasional Conformity*, to force Presbyterian mayors and common councilmen to attend parish churches during all their time of office. Had Queen Anne not died at this juncture the Toleration Act itself would have been repealed.

THE SUBSCRIPTION CONTROVERSY IN EXETER ASSEMBLY AND SALTERS' HALL, 1719.—By the accession of the House of Hanover in 1714 Presbyterians and other Nonconformists breathed more freely again, though this new-found liberty proved afterwards a snare; for the tendency of the age was toward all kinds of religious laxness, and the Presbyterians suffered sadly from this in many ways. A trying and adverse influence was exerted by some bitter contentions that broke out among them, especially a dangerous controversy about *Subscription to Articles of Faith*. In 1717 James Peirce, a noted and clever Presbyterian minister in Exeter, refused to state frankly his belief about the *Doctrine of the Trinity*; and in the Exeter Assembly (which was a Synod set up in 1655 by John Flavel and others to deal with matters of doctrine and discipline), while fifty-seven of the ministers subscribed the Article on the Trinity to show their soundness in the faith, as many as nineteen, or one-fourth of the whole, declined to be bound by any subscription. When the matter came before the famous SALTERS' HALL SYNOD in London, 1719, the same unhappy and violent division showed itself among all the Dissenters. The Presbyterian ministers, especially, broke up into three parties, vehemently opposed to each other—*Subscriptionists, Anti-Subscriptionists, and*

Neutrals—and this worked enormous damage to their cause in the eyes of the public.

DR. EDMUND CALAMY (born, 1671; died, 1732). The leader of the Neutrals, who, although a strong and orthodox Trinitarian, thought it a sad mistake to come to any vote on the matter, was the celebrated Dr. CALAMY, whose grandfather, father, himself and his son all bore the same honoured name—Edmund Calamy—and were all four of them, successively, Presbyterian ministers in London. The family was of Huguenot origin. His grandfather, the *first* Edmund was a foremost Presbyterian minister of his day, who took a leading part in the Westminster Assembly of Divines, and from whose house and hand came the great London "root and branch" petition to the Long Parliament against Prelacy in 1640. Both he and his son, the *second* Edmund, were among the noble ejected. And thus the *third* Edmund Calamy, commonly called for distinction Dr. Calamy, or Calamy *the younger*, had to go abroad to Holland for his education at the University of Utrecht. He settled in London, and ultimately, in a great meeting-house at Westminster, became, like his grandfather, the chief Presbyterian minister of his time. Among his many writings was the memorable "*Account of the Ejected Ministers, Lecturers, etc., of* 1662," a very precious and trustworthy record. His eldest son, the *fourth* Edmund Calamy, became a London minister, and died of consumption in 1755. Dr. Calamy himself was greatly distressed in his later years at the decay of vital religion, and at the serious defections and strife among his Presbyterian brethren.

INSIDIOUS TENDENCY TO ARIANISM AND ITS CAUSES, 1730-1760.—The Presbyterians had glided, or allowed themselves to be forced, into a false, or at least a treacherous, position. Presbyterian in name, they had ceased to be Presbyterially knit together. Their ministers were simply recognised in law as licensed religious teachers, and their meeting-houses were separately registered under particular trust-deeds, but the Presbyterian system had no legal standing and little development, save in individual congregations. When ministers, therefore, among them asserted their liberty to speculate about the Bible and its doctrines just as they pleased, there was no Presbyterial authority to restrain them or call them in question. For want of this, Arianism (the doctrine that disowns the Supreme Deity of our Lord and Saviour), or any other heresy that was fashionable, could silently and secretly work its way, especially in an age destitute of deep faith and warm personal love for the Saviour, when men made an idol of their liberty and were forgetful of its responsibilities. There were many other causes why the Presbyterians began to degenerate about 1735 and later, but the want of Presbyterial supervision was the chief; for thereby the sustaining and inspiriting influence that comes from mutual counsel was virtually lost. Organisation, indeed, is not life; but the highest life needs the best organisation; and, when this is lost or neglected, the life itself becomes a prey to every deadening influence. The Presbyterians were destined to suffer from this lack more than others.

UNHAPPY PREDICAMENT OF THE PRESBYTERIANS.—The state of the Law was very much to blame for the unfortunate condition of the Presbyterians. Other dissenting denominations were able under its protection to carry out their full system of worship and government. But this was not permitted to the Presbyterians, against whom some parts, both of civil and canon law, bore with peculiar hardship. Even the Toleration Act had less allowance for the Presbyterian system than for any of the others. It was one thing to tolerate a series of comparatively feeble and separate Assemblies for Protestant worship and discipline, and another thing to countenance a widespread and concerted organisation like the Presbyterians. Every movement in this direction was jealously watched as an infringement of the ecclesiastical jurisdiction, and of the rights and privileges of the ecclesiastical course. No doubt the Presbyterians might have done more in the way of common counsel and common action, so as, for example, to have controlled the teaching in their theological academies ; and this would have prevented many evils. But the cost of travel and correspondence then was great : congregations were strained to the utmost in keeping up what they felt most essential, the right and privilege of worshipping God according to conscience and in Protestant form: while the ministers showed, perhaps, more anxiety about personal maintenance and liberty than about the protection of the people from their own supineness and laxity. Thus " liberty," rather than "order and discipline," came naturally in the course of events to be their growing watchword : and this was strengthened by the mistaken notions many of them were tempted to entertain about creeds and subscription to Articles. Having been irritated and made to suffer under the religious tests imposed by civil authority, they had learned to cast themselves loose from all fixity of doctrine at a critical juncture, and gradually made light of every standard of orthodoxy or " pattern of sound words," lest they should seem to betray their rights and liberties. This proved a mistaken and fatal policy.

CHAPTER V.

Period of Defection and Decay, 1740-1800.

Depressed State of Religion in the Country.—The age of George I. and George II. was serviceable for political, mercantile, and other elements of material progress. But it was an age, unhappily, void of religious depth or earnestness. Previous struggles and party-collisions had been very favourable to the extension of liberty. Sacerdotal and other High-Church ideas were at a discount, and had themselves helped to bring about a materialistic reaction. As one has said: " A spiritual blight, affecting alike the interests of the truth and of religious life, for which many causes may be assigned, but which it is difficult to explain in any other way than by supposing the withdrawal of God's Spirit from the Churches of the Reformation, swept over the whole of Europe ". In England the period was characterised by fearful religious indifference, by low abandonment and licentiousness in morals, grossness of manners, corruption and profanity of speech. Presbyterian and other Puritanism was unable to cope with the fearful evils, and seemed content to creep quietly into corners and do its work without zeal or enthusiasm. All life and power seemed for the time to have gone out of it : and dearly did it pay the penalty of its unfaithfulness to truth and duty.

NATURE AND DRIFT OF THE ARIAN TENDENCY, 1735-1780.—It was the question of subscription to Articles of Faith over which Presbyterianism began to break into fragments, but while it was Arianism that became the fashionable heresy, any other doctrine might easily have taken its place. For the zeal of the non-subscribing, which was also the larger body of Presbyterian ministers, was not at first about doctrine, but about their right to uncontrolled freedom of religious inquiry and profession. Progress in error was slow at first, but after 1735 a number of prominent ministers, one in Birmingham, two in the Academy at Taunton, and several in London, began to teach free-and-easy opinions of an Arian kind. These men were all earnest for political and every other form of liberty. The Bible, too, they thoroughly believed in and reverenced; but ere long they began to regard it just as a field for free and boundless inquiry and speculation. With them saving faith was a mere assent to truths in doctrines and morals, and not a warm, living, personal trust in a living, personal Saviour. They gradually brought the Bible to their own standard of reason and common-sense, and forgot the need of the humbly sought teaching and illumination of the Holy Spirit of God, Christian Doctrine, thus ceasing to be real, downright conviction of soul, became with them a mere set or scheme of what they called "opinion". The great distinctive feature of these speculative Presbyterians was their constant boasting of "*free and candid religious inquiry*," as if men were to be "always learning and yet never come to an acknowledgment of the truth". Some of their early theological academies delighted in this principle of unrestricted freedom of speculating. So did such learned leaders among them as Dr. Nathaniel Lardner, Dr. Samuel Chandler, Dr. George Benson, and Dr. John Taylor, of

Norwich (who all died between 1760 and 1770). On these lines also the famous Academy at WARRINGTON became, from 1759 to 1786, an increasing fountain of unorthodox doctrine and activity.

SPIRITUAL DECAY AND PRESBYTERIAN DECREASE.—With growing laxity of doctrine came the still worse evil of religious indifference and lifelessness. Inward deadness bred outward decay. Presbyterians declined in numbers, vigour, and resources. Dissensions and panics paralysed their energy. By the middle of the century grand old Puritanism, both Presbyterian and Independent, seemed, if not an extinct, yet a sleeping volcano smothered in ashes. There seemed no earnest spiritual life anywhere. Not only was the National Church torpid, but it communicated its torpidity to others; and the clergy, left without discipline, were worldly, negligent, often immoral. Torrents of scepticism and irreligion flowed over the land. Christian divines wrote only books of apologies and defences of the faith; for a universal choke-damp was suffocating real vital godliness. The better endowed Presbyterian churches and the abler heterodox preachers drew curiously enough together. Many even who were trained as Independents, like Belsham and Dr. Priestley, became ministers of such Presbyterian charges. The word Presbyterian was thus getting to be associated with the unorthodox preachers, the others being called Independent in quite a haphazard, accidental and often mistaken way.

Some Presbyterian congregations which had been almost, became now altogether, Independent, as the best way to maintain their orthodoxy. Many congregations, both Presbyterian and Independent, became extinct under the general waning of religious life. The Presbyterians, however, suffered most: while in 1715 they were double the Independents, in 1772 there were 400 Independent congregations, with but 300 Presbyterian, and these about equally divided between orthodox and heterodox.

ARIANISM DRIVEN TO UNITARIANISM, 1780-1800.—A vast and startling development took place towards the close of the century. For fifty years cold and lifeless Arian preaching had been quietly and sleepily holding the field, emptying the meeting-houses. But the mighty upheavals of the French Revolution and the Methodist revival brought a new spirit into play. From Whitefield and Calvinistic Methodism fresh life poured into the old Independent congregations; but for Presbyterians the good time was not yet come. One of the chief Presbyterian representatives, Dr. Joseph Priestley, had with many others passed into Socinianism and Unitarianism, regarding Jesus as a mere Man, though a specially-endowed Messenger from God. In 1782 and 1786 he published elaborate works in defence of these views, vehemently challenging his former Arian position. This new Unitarian creed became fiercely aggressive and dogmatic, and began about 1790-4 to supplant the old Arianism. Thus at last the names Presbyterian and Unitarian came to be associated in the general mind. One thing, however, is clear, and never should be forgotten —that, however many of these old meeting-houses and endowments fell into Arian and Unitarian hands, the lapse and decay were not occasioned by Presbyterian polity or principles, but indeed by their absence. Such congregations were not really churches at all, but had long been simply a minister, trustees, and an audience, Unitarian in doctrine, and, though Presbyterian in name (for the sake of the old endowments or traditions), never Presbyterian in their practice.

PART III.

REVIVAL OF THE PRESBYTERIANS IN ENGLAND.

CHAPTER I.

Primary Period, 1672-1820.

SOURCES OF THE REVIVAL.—The recovery by the orthodox Presbyterians of their position in England has been one of the happy results of revived spiritual life, as their decline was a bitter fruit of spiritual deadness. While the bulk of the old meeting-houses had been passing under Arian and Unitarian influence, and some had died out or become Independent, a considerable number still remained faithful, especially in the northern counties and particularly in Northumberland. These old orthodox "meetings" obtained ministers from Scotland, or had their own students trained there; and thus a number of these venerable places were protected from heresy. Besides, there existed from an early date, especially in London, many purely *Scottish* Presbyterian congregations. As these grew and were more closely organised, they got the benefit of the Evangelical revival in Scotland, as well as of the great English Methodist movement, which was essentially a Presbyterian one, as we shall afterwards see.

FIRST SCOTTISH PRESBYTERIAN CHURCHES IN ENGLAND.
—The oldest of these was begun in FOUNDERS' HALL, London, so early as 1672. This was afterwards the church of LONDON WALL from 1764 to 1857, and is now the Presbyterian church in Canonbury. It has had many distinguished ministers, both English and Scotch, like Jeremiah Marsden, of Manchester, one of the ejected in 1662; Robert Fleming, author of *The Rise and Fall of the Papacy*; Principal Wishart, Dr. Henry Hunter, and several more of note. Other Scottish charges sprang up after the Revolution, like that of *Glasshouse Street*, which removed in 1710 to the French Protestant Church in *Swallow Street*, Piccadilly, where it was joined by most of the Swallow Street *English* Presbyterian Meeting which Baxter had founded in 1676; that in *Crown Court*, Drury Lane, in 1718, and that of *Peter Street*, Soho, in 1734. The ministers of these Scottish churches were associated with their English Presbyterian brethren in ordination proceedings, in the Merchants' Lecture, in the Salters' Hall Synod (as *Subscribers*), and in the general body of the Three Denominations who had a right of access to the Throne; and in various other ways. About the year 1760, however, they formed in London "THE SCOTS' PRESBYTERY," in self-defence against the non-subscribing or heterodox Presbyterian ministers.

SCOTTISH SECESSION CHURCHES. — Meanwhile another line of Scottish Presbyterian congregations, belonging to the SECESSION Church of Scotland, was being formed in England. The Secession arose thus: According to the Articles of the Treaty of Union between England and Scotland in 1707, the Presbyterian Church was to be maintained with all its rights and privileges as the National or Established Church in Scotland; and a special "Act of Security" for this was passed, requiring an oath to this effect from every sovereign on ascending the British throne. In five years, however, this was violated. For in 1712 an Act restoring patronage in the Scottish Church and depriving the people of their right to "call" or choose their own pastors was hurried through Parliament. Serious evils flowed from thus forcing ministers upon unwilling congregations. The cold wave of "Moderatism" (which was a mode of religion opposed at once to evangelical piety and to popular church administration) passed over Scotland; and it was the struggle that ensued which prevented Scottish Presbyterians from more effectually helping their orthodox brethren in England, and which delayed the Presbyterian revival. Out of this struggle arose the FIRST SECESSION or ASSOCIATE PRESBYTERY in Scotland, under the ERSKINES, in 1733. Through the high-handed measures of the "Moderate" majority in the General Assembly this movement rapidly advanced, with its earnest evangelical style of preaching on the one hand, and its demand for the freedom of congregations to call their own ministers on the other. So early as 1744 the Secession Church had obtained a foothold in England, in places so far apart as London and Newcastle, in both of which it had gathered some devout "praying societies" into settled congregations. Thus by the budding power and evangelic zeal of the Scottish Secession Church, as well as by the care of the Scottish National Church for its adherents in England, orthodox Presbyterianism took root again; and each of these sections was rallying to itself some of the old English Presbyterian meeting-houses.

FAITHFUL REMNANT OF ENGLISH PRESBYTERIAN CONGREGATIONS. — A good illustration of some of the old orthodox meetings, and how they became part of the present Presbyterian organisation, may be seen in the church at Stafford. Founded by the Rev. Noah Bryan, the ejected parish minister, in 1662, and struggling as a secret conventicle during the long persecution, this Presbyterian body was able to build a handsome meeting-house under the Toleration Act in 1689: it became connected with the Cheshire "Classis," of which John Angier was *Moderator* and Matthew Henry *Scribe* at its formation in 1691. After a goodly succession of ministers it began to feel difficulty in procuring suitable pulpit supply; but at the centenary in 1789 it secured a minister from Scotland, who saved it from Unitarian influence, and after him another who built up the cause; and then an Irish Presbyterian minister was obtained, under whom, in 1838, it joined the Lancashire Presbytery, which had been formed, as we shall see, some years before.

PRESBYTERIAN SURVIVAL IN THE NORTHERN COUNTIES, ESPECIALLY IN NORTHUMBERLAND.—Northumberland, with its seventy Presbyterian congregations (including those in Newcastle), has long been the most Presbyterian county in England. Here Presbyterianism in its orthodox form rooted itself as a native plant, when dying out elsewhere from the English soil. Here it had early associations with Aidan and the Church of Iona; with the preaching of John Knox, John Udall, Christopher Love, and Alexander Henderson; with the Newcastle *Classis* or Presbytery of 1648-1660, and with "Black Bartholomew" of 1662. Among the *thirty-eight* ejected ministers in Northumberland were HENRY ERSKINE, of Cornhill, father of the two famous founders of the Scottish Secession, Ebenezer and Ralph Erskine (an interesting and noteworthy link of connection between English and Scottish Presbyterians); LUKE OGLE, vicar of Berwick; and most eminent of all Dr. GILBERT RULE, vicar of Alnwick, who became Principal of Edinburgh University; and Dr. RICHARD GILPIN, who originated the *Newcastle Class* of 1693—the minutes of which we possess from 1751. Of the early Northumberland "meetings," now included in the Presbyterian Church of England, are Pottergate or St. James's, Alnwick, 1689; Morpeth, 1694; Stamfordham, Bavington, Etal, Lowick, Birdhope-Craig, and the Groat Market (now John Knox) Church, Newcastle, 1698, and others. The oldest *Secession* Church of Northumberland is that now in Blackett Street, Newcastle, which dates from 1744.

By 1836 we find no fewer than six Presbyteries of different kinds in Northumberland. How these have happily all become united under one Synod we shall afterwards see.

CHAPTER II.

PERIOD OF METHODIST DEVELOPMENT, 1735-1890.

HOW METHODISM UNDER WESLEY BECAME PRESBYTERIAN.—Methodism, a byword at first, soon grew by a certain fitness into a name of honour for one of the mightiest religious quickenings England has ever seen. It was the old Puritan spirit risen again from the dead, under new and more hopeful conditions, with a strong tendency to a Presbyterian form.

John Wesley a Presbyterian.—Its distinguished founder, John Wesley, himself was of Puritan descent on both sides. His great-grandfather, on the mother's side, was the famous Presbyterian "patriarch" of Dorchester, Rev. John White, while both great-grandfather and grandfather on the father's side were among the ejected ministers of 1662. His father, who had been trained as a Presbyterian student, and his mother, who was a daughter of the Presbyterian, Dr. Annesley (whose life was the first published writing of the Presbyterian Daniel Defoe), though they at last entered the Church of England, carried much of the Puritan spirit with them, like many others who have made the same transition. His mother especially, a remarkable woman, kindled a flame of spiritual fire and fervour in her husband's parish of Epworth, and transmitted her zeal to her sons.

Wesley's Methodism a Presbyterian Church.—The word Methodist has three historic phases—its first or University phase was devotional, after high-church or rubrical pattern; its second, or popular phase, was warmly evangelical and evangelistic; while its third, or "Society" phase, was Connexional, with a steady tendency towards the Presbyterial. And as it rolled along, the movement, by its spirit of zeal on the one hand, and its organised cohesion on the other, met exactly the two great wants of the age. It was in 1739 that Wesley first openly revolted from the Church of England, by refusing to obey the Bishop of Bristol, by preaching in the fields, and by founding the "Religious Societies" on a definite plan of his own. A few years later he had ceased to be a High-Churchman, had become theoretically Presbyterian from studying Lord Chancellor King's *Enquiry into the Primitive Church*, and declared in his Journal for January, 1746, that Episcopal succession was "a fable which no man ever did or could prove". He had already sent forth his "preachers," though he did not formally ordain any by laying on of hands till 1784, the year of the "Polldeed," or *Magna-Charta* of Methodism. In 1787, four years before his death, he put the Chapels and Societies for protection under the Act for *Dissenters*, and declared in memorable words: "As soon as I am gone the Methodists will be a regular Presbyterian Church". Time has confirmed the statement, and the Wesleyans are now a truly Presbyterian Church.

RISE OF THE CALVINISTIC METHODIST, OR PRESBYTERIAN CHURCH IN WALES.—The religious revival in Wales preceded that in England by a few years, although it derived its name from becoming attached to the doctrinal teaching of George Whitefield, rather than of John Wesley. But as Whitefield was a travelling Evangelist and not an organiser, Welsh

Methodism remained for half a century simply in the form of preaching and praying societies within the Established Church, and had no other ecclesiastical bond till its leaders were persecuted and at length thrust out of that Church altogether.

The Spiritual Awakening, 1735-1791.—The first religious awakening had begun in 1735 at three different centres in South Wales, under Howell Harris, Esq. of Trevecca, Rev. Daniel Rowlands of Llangeitho, Cardigan, and Rev. Howell Davies of Llysyfran, Pembrokeshire, these earnest young revivalists knowing nothing, however, for a time, of each other's work, nor of the parallel one in England. Among the fathers and founders of the Welsh Methodists were also the Rev. William Williams of Pantycelyn, who wrote their hymns, and the Rev. Peter Williams, whose Commentary is their family Bible. A spirit of alienation, which sprang up after a time between " Harris's people" and " Rowland's people" did much, with other causes, to check the movement; but a fresh revival in 1791, under the devoted Rev. THOMAS CHARLES of Bala, led to remarkable results. It was this good man's zeal for Sabbath and " circulating " schools that led, as everyone knows, to the formation of the British and Foreign Bible Society, by which Wales alone was supplied with 100,000 Scriptures in ten years.

The Presbyterian Organisation, 1811.—Through Mr. Charles's influence, an "Order of Government and Rules of Discipline" for the Societies came into use in 1801; but he and other episcopally ordained clergymen among the Methodists shrank from separation from the Established Church as long as they could avoid it. It was not till 1811 the decisive step was taken, which Wesley had taken nearly twenty years earlier, of organising the Connection Presbyterially, and ordaining preachers and investing them with full pastoral functions. In 1823 a "Confession of Faith" was adopted, but it was only in 1864 that the two Associations of North and South Wales were merged in one "General Assembly," and the title "Presbyterian Church" began to be used. This may be regarded as really *the* Church of the Welsh people. It need hardly be said how powerfully these Methodist movements in England and Wales have told in favour of Presbyterian principles.

CHAPTER III.

Period of Presbyterial and Synodical Organisation, 1820-1843.

EVANGELICAL PRESBYTERIANISM ORGANISING ITSELF.—Under the fostering zeal of the Scottish SECESSION, as well as of the NATIONAL CHURCH of Scotland, orthodox evangelical Presbyterianism began again to spread its roots in England. Both these sections of Presbyterians held fast by the Westminster Standards of doctrine and government, though with minor differences of administration, and each of them managed to rally to itself a number of the distinctively English Presbyterian charges.

In connection with the Scottish Secession.—The Secession Church of Scotland which had obtained a foot-hold in London and Newcastle in 1744, had so grown in 1820 as to be able to erect a Presbytery in each of these cities; a third one was formed in Lancashire in 1831, as the outcome of the two mother churches there—Lloyd Street, Manchester, founded in 1798, and Mount Pleasant, Liverpool, in 1801. So early as 1792 Graham of Newcastle had published his notable *Review of Ecclesiastical Establishments in Europe*, which opened the great modern question of the freedom of religion from State patronage and control. This led afterwards to the "voluntary" controversy which produced much bitter strife and alienation between the Presbyterian parties and widened their separation for a time.

In connection with the Church of Scotland.—Meanwhile the Scottish National Church, with an increase of evangelical power after 1812, had been very helpful in training and providing preachers for many of the old northern orthodox and native Presbyterian congregations, while numbers of those who had been reared in her communion and who preferred her worship and government, were engaged in raising up new Churches of her order in great centres, like those of *Oldham Street* and *Rodney Street*, Liverpool; *St. Peter's, Grosvenor Square*, Manchester; and especially *Regent Square*, London, which was built for EDWARD IRVING, in 1827. It was in 1836 that the newly-formed Lancashire Presbytery of this section of the Church joined with the North-west of England Presbytery in forming a Synod, according to the advice of the GENERAL ASSEMBLY of the Church of Scotland.

AN ENGLISH SYNOD FORMED IN CONNECTION WITH THE CHURCH OF SCOTLAND—Thus in 1836, a Synod was formed in England on a separate and independent footing, in close ecclesiastical Communion no doubt with the Church of Scotland, but never a portion of its organisation nor subject to its jurisdiction. This ENGLISH SYNOD was completed in 1842 by the gradual adhesion to it of the old London Presbytery and that of Newcastle-on-Tyne, both in 1839; of Berwick in 1840; of Northumberland and of North-west Northumberland in 1842—seven Presbyteries in all, with sixty-three congregations. It is worth noticing that of these sixty-three congregations composing the Synod as many as two-thirds were of old English Presbyterian origin (thirty-five of them dating even from before 1750);

about eighteen of the same class were already connected with the Secession Church.

FAVOURING CIRCUMSTANCES. While the orthodox or evangelical Presbyterians were thus struggling into organisation, certain favourable circumstances helped them. We select the following three: (1) Since the Revolution of 1688 the representatives of the three denominations—Presbyterian, Independent, and Baptist—had a joint right of access to the throne with petitions or addresses; and in 1727 their several Boards formed themselves into a "General Body" for certain practical purposes. The Unitarian members withdrew in 1836, after doctrinal views had been hotly debated for many years among its constituents; but as there were by this time several evangelical Presbyterians in the "General Body," *they* were now declared by the other members to be the true Presbyterian representatives for the purposes for which the "General Body" existed. Thus the Evangelical Presbyterians secured a new foothold, by wresting from the Unitarians this important position. (2) But what chiefly depressed the Unitarian interest was the great legal decision of 1842 in the Lady Hewley case. Lady Hewley, widow of Sir John Hewley, Lord Mayor of York, had left large estates in the hands of seven trustees, orthodox Presbyterians like herself, on behalf of "poor and godly preachers of Christ's Holy Gospel," and for kindred objects. The Trusts came into operation at her death in 1710, but in the course of the century they fell into the hands of Unitarian administrators. After a twelve years' Chancery suit, from 1830 to 1842, the House of Lords finally decreed that the Unitarian trustees must be removed, and their place be taken by three evangelical Presbyterians, two Independents, and two Baptists, to manage the chief trust for their respective denominations. The Unitarians, struck with dismay at the insecure tenure of their old meeting-houses and endowments of Presbyterian foundation, obtained from Parliament the "Chapel Act" of 1844, and thus appealed to law rather than equity for the maintenance of the disputed property. (3) Other circumstances, especially their extreme fluctuations in doctrinal speculation, and their adoption of modern "free-thought," indicated the Unitarians' loss of prestige, while, at the same time, the long-depressed evangelical or orthodox Presbyterians plucked up fresh courage and made new advances.

CHAPTER IV.

Period of Quickening and Increase, 1843-1876.

FRESH IMPULSES IN 1843 AND 1847.—The growing influence of the Evangelical party in the Scottish NATIONAL CHURCH had all along lent an impulse to the Presbyterian cause in England. This was immensely increased, however, after the "ten years' conflict," when the struggle for spiritual independence had issued in the DISRUPTION of 1843, and Dr. Chalmers and 474 of his brethren surrendered their manses, glebes, and stipends, to the amount of at least £100,000 per annum, and proceeded to organise THE FREE CHURCH relying on the good-will offerings of the people. With this stirring movement the SYNOD IN ENGLAND heartily sympathised; and, although eighteen congregations still preferred to continue "in connection with the Church of Scotland," (and formed a SYNOD, having under its jurisdiction four Presbyteries, with eighteen ministers in charges, and sixteen army chaplains), the main Synod, with sixty-three congregations still under its charge, took up a self-reliant position, and under the simpler and more accurate name of "THE PRESBYTERIAN CHURCH IN ENGLAND," without reference to any "connection with the Church of Scotland," resolved to carry on its Gospel work among English people, as well as among Scottish people on English soil.

THE PRESBYTERIAN CHURCH IN ENGLAND, 1843.—In proof of its new-born energy, the Presbyterian Church in England founded without delay, in 1844, a Theological College in London for training a native Presbyterian ministry, and in 1847 it set itself to its great FOREIGN MISSION WORK IN CHINA, with the devoted and apostolic WILLIAM C. BURNS as its first missionary. Nor should it be forgotten that the *Irish Presbyterian* ministers and congregations in England cast in their lot with this Church, which steadily grew during the next thirty years from sixty-three to one hundred and fifty-six congregations, its London Presbytery alone advancing from six to fifty-six congregations within the same period. Among specially prominent men in this section of the Church were Professor Hugh Campbell, who did good service during the Lady Hewley lawsuit; Principal Lorimer; Professor Thomas M'Crie, D.D., LL.D.; Dr. James Hamilton, with his three elders, Alex. Gillespie, James Nisbet, and Professor Leone Levi; Dr. Munro of Manchester, and his liberal-handed elder, Robert Barbour, Esq., whose benefactions and general services to Presbyterianism in England can never be over-estimated.

WILLIAM C. BURNS AND THE CHINA MISSION, 1847.— The beneficial influence of its China mission on the spiritual life of the Presbyterian Church in England was very marked and noteworthy. How singularly favoured it was in its first agent! The name of William Burns may be fitly mentioned in the same breath with Aidan, the apostle of Northumbria, Eliot, apostle to the Indians, and kindred apostolic men of the highest type of devotedness. Coming of a clerical family, being third son of "the pastor of Kilsyth," the remarkable work he did in his early years as a powerful evangelist and revival preacher especially in M'Cheyne's Church, Dundee, and throughout Scotland, in Newcastle-on-Tyne, in Dublin, and Canada, was a splendid preparation for his China labours. When asked by the Synod, on his ordination in Sunderland in 1847, how soon he could start, he is said to have replied, with prompt decision, "To-morrow," as he held up his little travelling bag. And within a few weeks he was on his way to China, in the spirit of its first Protestant missionary, Dr. Robert Morrison of "Dictionary" fame, who had been sent out in 1806 by the London Missionary Society, and who, it is interesting to note, was son of a Presbyterian elder in Newcastle-on-Tyne, and was ordained in Swallow Street Presbyterian Church, London. Morrison died in 1834, after vainly trying to secure a settlement in the country. It was not till 1842 that Europeans were allowed to reside in the five open ports; and of this and other slowly-acquired privileges William Burns took full advantage. The "memoir" of his life and labours must be consulted for details of his noble and peculiar work in founding a Christian community, and providing them with hymns and the beginning of a sacred literature in his translation of the *Pilgrim's Progress*. His consecrated life was spent in apostolic simplicity. We read: "A small house was rented for him at 2s. 6d. a month. Here he lived for four years." Again: "The room in which he died had but few comforts, certainly no luxuries. The form on which he slept, a table, two chairs, two book-cases, and a foreign stove, made up the furniture." He moved about like his Master, in sublime and dignified superiority to his material surroundings; fulfilling his own ideal in the oft-quoted words: "The happiest state of a Christian on earth seems to be to have few wants".

THE UNITED PRESBYTERIAN CHURCH AND ITS ENGLISH SYNOD, 1847.—Meanwhile the other section of Presbyterians, the SECESSION, had been also making advances under its new name, THE UNITED PRESBYTERIAN CHURCH, which had been adopted in 1847, on its joining with the SYNOD OF RELIEF (*i.e.*, from patronage), a body which had left the Church of Scotland in 1752, because of the intolerable working of the mischievous Patronage Act of 1712. Much good flowed from this union, the United Presbyterians steadily increasing to 620 congregations in the three kingdoms, and raising during the next thirty years (1847 to 1876) about £7,000,000, a tenth of this large sum being for foreign missions. In England their congregations doubled from fifty to a hundred, so that, in 1867, a special ENGLISH SYNOD of the United Presbyterian Church was created, with a view to further progress. Among prominent ministers in this section of the Church in England may be mentioned Drs. Jerment, Waugh, Archer, King, and MacFarlane, of London; Drs. Jack and M'Kerrow, of Manchester; Dr. George Young, the geologist and topographer, of Whitby; Drs. Stewart, Crighton, and Professor Graham, of Liverpool, with many other active ministers and elders.

CAUSES OF PRESBYTERIAN SEPARATION.—What kept these two parties, the PRESBYTERIAN CHURCH in ENGLAND and the ENGLISH SYNOD of the UNITED PRESBYTERIANS, so long asunder was their different origin and history, but especially the alienation occasioned by the vehement "Voluntary Controversy," which raged from 1830 to 1850 on the proper relations of Church and State and on the whole question of the civil magistrate's duty towards the Christian Conscience. Could no escape be found from such difficulties and more Presbyterian union be promoted?

DR. JAMES HAMILTON AND MOVEMENTS FOR UNION.—So

early as 1849 Dr. James Hamilton, with other kindred spirits, was pressing this question forward, though he did not himself live to see the much-desired union accomplished.

Dr. HAMILTON, who was born in Paisley, 1814, and died in London, 1867, after fifty-three years of very busy and nobly-spent life, did much for Evangelical Presbyterianism in England. Receiving a careful training in the happy home of Strathblane, where his father, Dr. William Hamilton, was parish minister, and distinguishing himself in his early student's career by literary, botanical, and theological attainments, James Hamilton came thoroughly equipped as minister to Regent Square Church in 1841, and did splendid and varied service there by his preaching, his pen, and, above all, by his genial and gracious personality. A man of high spiritual character, and of the most catholic disposition, who greatly delighted in labouring for the Evangelical Alliance and all good Christian causes, he took a foremost part in every enterprise of the section of the Church to which by preference he belonged, whether lecturing in its college, editing its monthly periodical, or directing its young and notable China Mission. Few names can be dearer to the Presbyterian Church of England than that of James Hamilton. His "*Life in Earnest,*" his "*Happy Home,*" and other series of tracts, his "*Christian Classics,*" and many more of his books will long continue to "praise him in the gate".

CHAPTER V.

Period of Consolidation and Extension, 1876-1891.

The Union of 1876. "The Presbyterian Church of England" Constituted. — For ten long years, from 1863 to 1873, negotiations had been in progress in Edinburgh for an incorporative union between the Free, the United Presbyterian, the Reformed Presbyterian, and the English Presbyterian Churches. These larger negotiations having however failed, an effort was made to secure their benefit on a smaller scale, south of the Tweed. This effort proved successful: and an important chapter was added to Presbyterian history in England by the union between the Synod of the "Presbyterian Church in England" and the English Synod of the "United Presbyterian Church". On the 13th June, 1876, both Synods met in Liverpool, and, proceeding from their respective places of meeting, they mingled in one as they entered together the Philharmonic Hall, where this union of Presbyterians on English soil was formally inaugurated, and the joint-synod constituted under its new or slightly-altered name, "The Presbyterian Church *of* England," and presided over by its venerable first moderator, Rev. Dr. James Anderson, of Morpeth.

The Presbyterian Church of England. — This

Church claims to be *Scriptural* in constitution, *Apostolic* in government, worship and financial administration, *Evangelical* in doctrine, *Missionary* in aim, and truly *Catholic* in spirit, bound to cherish the most loving regard for every faithful branch of the Christian Church throughout the world, and to say from the heart: "Grace be with all them that love our Lord Jesus Christ in sincerity".

Its Constitution.—It holds the word of God, in the Scriptures of the Old and New Testaments, to be the supreme authoritative rule of faith and duty, both for the individual and for the Church. The Church's subordinate standards of doctrine are the WESTMINSTER CONFESSION and CATECHISMS. These are purely English books. They are not imposed on church members, but are employed to protect the Church from crude or false doctrine on the part of her public teachers, and to guarantee the befitting qualifications and conduct of all her office-bearers, as well as guard their rights in the discharge of duty. "The Church of God is regarded as essentially a spiritual institution, constituted by a heavenly calling, and owning allegiance in her proper sphere to none but the Lord Jesus Christ. Presbyterians do not admit the ecclesiastical supremacy of the Crown of England. While honouring the jurisdiction of the State over civil affairs, they hold the internal administration of the Church for her proper spiritual work to be distinct from civil rule, and quite outside the sphere of Crown and Parliament." The Constitution of the Presbyterian Church of England, and the usual Rules and Forms of its Procedure, may be learned from "THE BOOK OF ORDER," published in 1883, and issued more recently with revisions and additions; while all other details may be found in the annual "Blue-Book," containing the Synod's minutes and the reports of its committees.

Its Polity and Administration.—As a branch of the visible Church it holds the Presbyterian form of government, which it regards as "founded on and agreeable to the Word of God," and as substantially the mode of government prevailing in apostolic times. It needs no officers but such as are expressly named in the New Testament, and these are chosen by its own members, as in Apostolic times. Moreover, it is the form of government which was adopted by nearly all the Reformed Churches when they cast off the corruptions of popery—the prelacy retained in the English Church being exceptional. The Presbyterian mode of church-government is more widely diffused and accepted than any other in Protestant Christendom. The apostles appointed "bishops" or "elders" in "every Church"; and it is now recognised that "elders" and "bishops" were the same, the word "bishops" or "overseers" having special reference to the *duties*, and "elders" to the *rank* of the office. Church government is thus committed to bodies of teaching and ruling elders, all duly elected by the members of the Church. Elders of a single congregation meeting together, with the minister, are commonly called a "session," the "deacons" or managers being their helpers in the financial, charitable, and other outward or secular affairs of the Church. The meeting of the ministers or preaching elders with the representative elders of a number of congregations in any locality is called a "Presbytery"; and ministers who are chosen by the people are ordained and set in office by "the laying on of the hands of the Presbytery". A meeting of elders or bishops over a wider area is commonly called a "Synod" or an "Assembly". The chairman who presides over any of these meetings is known as the "Moderator". By such a popular and representative government, with its gradations of meetings or "courts" in the "Lord's House," provision is made for all things being done "decently and in order": the rights and liberties of members are preserved and guarded, discipline and purity are maintained, and vigorous administration secured. Church government is not, however, empowered, like secular government, to make and impose laws of its own devising, but only to administer the rule of Christ, and to do this in His own name and in His own spirit. Thus the Church of Christ is a spiritually independent and self-governing body, civil power being wholly excluded.

Its Doctrine. — Its system of doctrine is Evangelical, drawn wholly from Scripture, and is embodied in the Westminster Confession and Catechisms of 1646—which have been retained, with modifications, by the English-speaking Presbyterian Church everywhere throughout the world as its creed. This is in all essentials the same as the other confessions or symbolic books of the Churches of the Reformation in its interpretation of "the faith once delivered to the saints". But as it is the duty of every Church to express its "pattern of sound words" in the current language of the people, and to lay emphasis on aspects of the truth specially demanded by the times, the Presbyterian Church of England has for popular use set forth its teaching in twenty-four brief and simple "Articles of the Faith," which were accepted with absolute unanimity by the Synod of 1890, as an approved statement of the Church's doctrine. These articles declare that there is one living and true God; and that in the unity of the ever-blessed Godhead there is a personal distinction of Father, Son, and Holy Ghost, equal in power and glory, without any division of substance; and that this is the very God of Creation, of Providence, and of Redemption. That all mankind, originally made in God's image and existing in Adam as their first parent and representative head, fell through him into a state of sin and misery, from which no man is able to deliver himself. That the only but all-sufficient Saviour provided by the matchless love of God is the Lord Jesus Christ, who, by His perfect obedience and atoning death, has accomplished eternal redemption for us: that lost sinners of mankind must put their trust in him as their Saviour, voluntarily, yet not without the help of Divine grace, so as to accept the free and gracious offer of pardon, peace, and purifying power at His hands: and that by the solemn call of the Gospel every individual sinner is bound, warranted, and welcome to do so. Those united thus to Christ by a living faith are the elect of God, who, being regenerated by the Holy Spirit, as well as justified by His grace, are rendered spiritually and persistently obedient to God's holy law and will as it is authoritatively set forth in sacred Scripture. All who are or profess to be Christian should join together in the public worship, ordinances, and fellowship of the Church: should seek the prosperity and extension of Christ's kingdom on earth: and should ever be looking and preparing for the Lord's coming in judgment, so as to be among the holy and happy company of the redeemed in glory.

Its Worship.—While strongly inculcating private and family worship in the home, the Presbyterian Church of England loves a simple, sober and intelligent form of public worship, with various adaptations to the state of culture and taste among her members, as may be seen in the *Revised Directory for the Public Worship of God* and in her book of *Church Praise*, which has received such wide-spread currency and the highest commendations. Public worship consists of common prayer and praise, with preaching and reading and hearing of the Word of God, and the administration from time to time of the Ordinances of Baptism and the Lord's Supper. The general order is the one laid down, with no small care and thought, in the Westminster *Directory*, which has been followed by all sections of English-speaking Protestants who do not use a Liturgy, though not in itself contrary to the use of stated or prepared forms of prayer. It proceeds, however, on the principle that prayer is a free and gracious gift of God's Spirit which must be stirred up into lively exercise by both ministers and people, through meditation, and a painstaking use of a growing spiritual experience and Christian attainment. Those who drew it up were men of great devotion and eminent abilities in prayer, who, in pleading at a throne of grace, could move and melt the hearts of others, and sought to rouse their desires to the exercise of the same spiritual and heavenly gift. Presbyterian Church service admits of no material altar, nor of any sacerdotal class or caste. All its members are priests, and its sacrifices are those of prayer, praise, and personal oblation. It makes much of the preaching of the Cross, and nothing of its mere external use and pageantry. Believing the visible Church to consist of all who make a credible profession of faith in Christ together with their children, it admits the latter to Baptism, just as it remembers them in its prayers. It is also a recognised portion of public worship to offer of our substance to the service of God Festivals of commemoration, because they lack scriptural authority, are not to be enforced like the Lord's day nor held as binding on the Christian conscience. All public services of the Church are to be regulated by the New Testament and conducted with due solemnity, without burdensome ceremonial and in the known tongue of the people.

Its General Work.—The Presbyterian Church of England does its general or common work under seven main schemes —The SUSTENTATION FUND, HOME MISSIONS, FOREIGN MISSIONS, JEWISH MISSIONS, CONTINENTAL WORK, COL-

LEGE, and INSTRUCTION OF YOUTH. These schemes are carried on, not through separate societies, but as actual parts of the Church's organisation: the funds raised for these different objects being carefully administered by responsible committees of office-bearers, under the immediate inspection and control of the Synod.

Sustentation Fund.—The object of this fund is the worthy and adequate support of an efficient Gospel ministry in all parts of the Church. Here the New Testament principle, that the strong should help the weak, is brought into play—the strong congregations which draw many of their *members* from the smaller congregations, giving to them in turn out of their larger *substance*. The working basis of the fund is, that a self-supporting congregation may supplement its own minister's stipend after sending in to the fund the *equal dividend* of £200 or more. The great bulk of the congregations are, of course, self-supporting. Twenty-five contribute a little to the fund and take nothing out. Five of the wealthier aid-giving congregations pay a total of more than £3000 into the fund, and receive £1000 out. Ninety-eight are aid-receiving; twenty-four of these not being on the equal dividend platform. To be on this equal dividend platform no congregation may send less than £110 per annum. If a congregation can only send £80—and no congregation can send less and be a participant—it receives £155: but as an encouragement to exertion, whatever additional sum it sends, it receives back with one-half more added. The basis of arrangements with assisted congregations is revised every three years: so simple and self-adjusting is its working.

Missions.—The HOME MISSION scheme has two objects. (1) To raise and administer funds for church building or reduction of building debt. The value of churches, manses, and other buildings, which was estimated at one million sterling at the time of the union in 1876, is now increased in 1890 to upward of a million and a half; while the debt, which at the former date, amounted to £120,000, is now reduced to £82,000. (2) The other most urgent object of this fund is to promote and further Evangelistic and Home Missionary efforts—a matter of very vital and vast importance, in which much remains to be done in stimulating earnest and loving Christian work among all classes. Of the Church's FOREIGN MISSIONS the first in time and importance is that to China, which is one of the most remarkable of modern missionary enterprises. Begun by the saintly and apostolic William Burns only in 1847, it has now a membership of upwards of 6000 in 134 congregations gathered from heathenism in the five localities of Amoy, Swatow, Hak-ka country, Formosa, and Singapore, with more than one hundred native preachers, eight native pastors entirely supported by their own congregations, and fifty students under theological training—and it is steadily becoming a self-governing, self-supporting and self-propagating Church. Already the business of the three local Presbyteries is conducted in Chinese; native ministers and elders taking part. Already eight native pastors are entirely supported by their own congregations; and native missions in the Pescadores and elsewhere are now being maintained by the Chinese themselves. Even already, our native Chinese agents out-number the Europeans by two to one. Meanwhile there are forty-six missionary agents from this country variously at work; twenty of these being ordained ministers, nine medical missionaries, three teachers, and fourteen lady missionaries, supported by themselves or by the "Women's Missionary Association". The progress of the mission has been in every way striking. Fourteen years ago, in 1876, there were, for example, only two hospitals; now, in 1891, there are ten, with an average of 3000 patients in a year: and while in 1876 there was no native Christian press at work, now one station alone issues nearly 300,000 pages a year. The Church has also a small but thriving INDIAN MISSION at Rampore Bauleah, while its JEWISH MISSION is zealously carried on in London and in Morocco. Aid is extended also in some measure to a number of struggling Free Protestant Churches on THE CONTINENT, specially the Waldensian and Free Italian Churches. The total missionary contributions for 1890 amounted to nearly £23,000, or about one-tenth of the Church's general income.

Education and Educational Work.—The Presbyterian Church has always been distinguished for its educated ministry. It has insisted on years of special training and on a thorough equipment for such responsible work. It will "lay hands suddenly on no man" and admits "no novice". A most important institution, therefore, is its THEOLOGICAL COLLEGE, presided over by Principal Dykes, D.D., and his colleagues, Professors John Gibb, D.D., and John Skinner, M.A., with twenty to thirty students, a large and valuable library, and a number of both undergraduate and theological scholarships. Popular religious education has also ever been a special care with the Presbyterian Church. Whatever duties it recognises as belonging to the State, and whatever responsibilities belong primarily to the parent, it has ever as a Church acted on the great call and requirement of the Master: "Feed my Lambs," as well as "Feed my Sheep". Like other Churches, it makes provision for the religious tuition of its little ones, and for directing and stimulating this sacred work. Its committee for the INSTRUCTION OF YOUTH is the latest but not the least deserving of its schemes for the retention of the young people, and training them to high and intelligent service.

Its Growth and Position.—The slow but sure and steady advance of the Presbyterian Church of England may be gathered from the following statistics. At the union in 1876 it had 270 congregations, 50,000 members, ten presbyteries, and an income of £163,000. In 1888 it had 288 congregations, 62,000 members, eleven presbyteries, and an income of £200,000, which grew to £210,000 in 1889, to £235,000 in 1890, and to about £240,000 at the last return, with a corresponding increase of congregations and members. Elders, deacons and managers now number upwards of 5000, or one in every thirteen of the church members, the elders being one in every thirty-five. There are nearly 80,000 Sabbath scholars, under about 8000 teachers, who with district visitors, Dorcas Society members, and other male and female Christian workers, constitute nearly a fourth of the membership of the Church. There is need for all.

Besides "The Book of Order" and other publications of the Church's Committee, special mention may be made of its periodicals;—*The Presbyterian Messenger*, weekly; the *Messenger and Missionary Record*, monthly; the *Children's Messenger*, illustrated, monthly; and *Our Sisters in other Lands*, quarterly, on behalf of the Women's Missionary Association.

While cultivating the most brotherly and friendly spirit toward every other Christian denomination, the Presbyterian Church of England stands in closest federal relations with the Free and United Presbyterian Churches, and is in sympathetic touch with all the Presbyterian Churches of the world by means of their "General Alliance".

THE GENERAL ALLIANCE AND VAST EXTENT OF PRESBYTERIANISM.—One of the happiest and most prominent features of modern Presbyterianism is the spirit of union it is manifesting in its various branches throughout the world. The most conspicuous evidence of this is the formation of the great Pan-Presbyterian Council or Alliance of Presbyterian Churches all over the world. This organisation sprang into being at an International Conference, which was held in the London Presbyterian College, in July, 1875. The first general council of this Alliance met in Edinburgh, in July, 1877; the second in Philadelphia, in September, 1880; the third in Belfast, in 1884; the fourth, a very important one, in London, in 1888, on the tercentenary of the destruction of the Armada, and the bi-centenary of the Revolution of 1688; and the fifth is to meet in Toronto, Canada, in 1892. Delegates from fifty Presbyterian bodies in twenty-five different countries, speaking many different languages, representing twenty thousand congregations, four million communicants, and twenty million adherents, meet together in this Alliance for common counsel. The statistics of so vast a body of Presbyterian Churches in many lands, and in all quarters of the globe, must enlighten such as are under the mistaken notion that Presbyterianism is a small and chiefly a Scottish mode of worship and government, and may surprise even those who are not wholly unaware of its world-wide diffusion. The Presbyterian system of representative Church government, securing faith without superstition, cohesion without coercion, order without tyranny, and liberty without caprice, prevails in some of the most powerful and progressive Churches of modern Christendom.

CONCLUSION.—Presbyterianism has thus done much toward the solution of some delicate and difficult problems, such as that of a Free Church in a Free State, and a free conscience in a free, Evangelical, and international Church system. Even in England, though its influence has been comparatively small, it has not been unfruitful of good. All along the line of its history it helped to give a more emphatic turn and tone to the Protestantism of England. Twice over it sacrificed itself for the good of the nation : first, by hasting to restore Charles II. so as to save the nation from anarchy ; and then, by declining the bribes of James II. so as to protect Church and State from his popery and tyranny. And even while barely tolerated, and while in subjection to such severely repressive measures as the Test and the Corporation Acts, its adherents in town-councils were among the stoutest defenders of municipal and local self-government. Its own free and representative government has been, moreover, in fuller and happier accord with the genius of the English constitution than any other form of Church polity in the nation. Even in its decline and eclipse it did much for English freedom, and certainly paved the way for the puritan and religious revival in Methodism. It led the van too in England in the matter of Christian giving and liberality, and helped to show how religious worship and ordinances might be maintained and extended, as in the Primitive Church, by the free-will offerings of the people. There is still room and need for a Presbyterian Church in the midst of the English people : and, if only wise and faithful to its trust, the Presbyterian Church of England may be enabled, by the Divine blessing, to verify further the old historic Presbyterian badge—the burning bush with its motto, "*nec tamen consumebatur*".

Books of Reference.

1. HISTORY.

Baxter's Life and Times. From his own Manuscripts. 1696.
History of the Puritans 1517 to 1688]. By Daniel Neal. 4 vols. 1732-1738.
The Nonconformist's Memorial. By Edmund Calamy, D.D., and Samuel Palmer. 2 vols. 1775.
Lives of the Puritans. By Benjamin Brook. 3 vols. 1813.
Westminster Assembly, History of. By W. M. Hetherington, D.D., LL.D., 1843, and by Prof. A. F. Mitchell, D.D., 1883. **Minutes of** (Nov., 1644, to March, 1649). Edited by Drs. Mitchell and Struthers, 1874.
Annals of English Presbytery. By Thomas M'Crie, D.D., LL.D. 1872.
History of Religion in England. [1640 to 1880.] By John Stoughton, D.D. 7 vols. 1881.
History of the Presbyterians in England. By Rev. A. H. Drysdale, M.A. 1889.

2. EARLIER PUBLIC DOCUMENTS.

Admonition to Parliament. 1572.
Ecclesiasticæ Disciplinæ Explicatio. By Walter Travers. 1574.
The Directory of Church Government. [By Thomas Cartwright and others. Published 1644, and reprinted 1872.
Westminster Assembly's Documents: viz., The Directory for Public Worship, 1644; The Doctrinal Part of the Ordination of Ministers, 1644; The Presbyterial Form of Church Government, 1645; The Confession of Faith, 1646; The Shorter Catechism, 1647; The Larger Catechism, 1648.
Jus Divinum Regiminis Ecclesiastici. By sundry Ministers in London. 1647.
A Vindication of the Presbyterial Government. 1649. } By the Provincial
Jus Divinum Ministerii Evangelici. 1654. } Assembly of London.

3. DOCUMENTS OF THE MODERN PERIOD.

Digest of the Proceedings of Synod of the Presbyterian Church in England, 1836-1876. By Leone Levi, LL.D. 1877.
Minutes of the Synod of the Presbyterian Church of England, with Committee's Reports. (Annually.) 1876, &c.
The Presbyterian Church of England: an Outline of its Doctrine, &c. By Donald Fraser, D.D. 1877.
The Book of Order of the Presbyterian Church of England. 1883.
The Westminster Directory for Public Worship. Revised by a Committee of the Synod of the Presbyterian Church of England. 1890.
The Articles of the Faith, approved by the Synod of the Presbyterian Church of England. 1890.

Index of Names.

Note.— For *subjects* (*e.g.*, Methodism, the Prophesyings, Presbytery in Lancashire and in America, etc., etc.), consult the Table of Contents, to which this Index is supplementary.

	PAGE
Act against Occasional Conformity,	86
— against Schism,	86
— Chapel,	106
— Conventicle,	71
— Corporation,	79
— Five Mile,	71
— of Security,	95
— of Supremacy,	28
— of Toleration,	78, 80, 86
— of Uniformity,	28, 29, 70
— Oxford,	71
— Test,	79
"Admonition, The,"	36
Aelfric,	18
Aidan,	17
A'Lasco, John,	23
Alnwick, St. James's,	98
Anderson, James,	112
Angier, John,	97
Annesley, Samuel,	99
Anselm,	18
Archer, Thomas,	110
Arrowsmith, John,	49
Augustine,	16
Bancroft, Richard,	45
Barbour, Robert,	108
Bates, William,	70
Bavington,	98
Baxter, Richard,	65, 66, 69, 70, 71

	PAGE
Baynes, Paul,	42
Belsham, Thomas,	92
Benson, George,	91
Birdhope-Craig,	98
Bolton, Robert,	42
Book of Common Order,	27
— Martyrs,	27
— Order,	113
Bradshaw, Thomas,	40
Breda, Declaration of,	68, 69
Brook, Lord,	48
Bryan, Noah,	96
Bucer, Martin,	22
Burgess, Cornelius,	48
Burns, William C.,	108
Butler, Joseph,	85
Byfield, Adoniram,	49
Calamy, Edmund,	46, 49, 69, 70
Calamy, Dr. Edmund,	71, 81, 87
Calamy, Edmund,	87
"Call to the Unconverted,"	66
Calvin, John,	29
Cambridge Platform,	60
Campbell, Hugh,	108
Cartwright, Thomas,	32, 36, 37, 40, 42
Catechism, Larger,	54, 113
Catechism, Shorter,	54, 113
Cawdrey, Robert,	40
Chadderton, Lawrence,	40, 45
Chandler, Samuel,	91

Channel Islands,	37
Charles, Thomas,	101
Columba, St.,	17
Comprehension Bill,	78
Confession of Faith,	53, 113
Covenant, Solemn League and,	49, 59, 65
Coverdale, Miles,	27, 29, 30
Crighton, Hugh,	110
Cranmer, Thomas,	22
Davies, Howell,	101
Defoe, Daniel,	82, 99
D'Ewes, Sir Simonds,	48
Directory, The Presbyterian,	37, 39
Directory for Public Worship,	49
"Divine Right of the Gospel Ministry, The,"	59
Doctrinal Puritans,	42
Doctrinal Statement, Brief,	55
Dod, John,	40, 45
Doolittle, Thomas,	83
Dykes, J. Oswald,	120
Eliot, John,	60
Engagement, The,	65
"Enquiry," The,	79, 100
Erskine, Ebenezer,	96, 97
Erskine, Henry,	97
Erskine, Ralph,	96, 97
Essex, Earl of,	48
Etal,	98
"Faerie Queen,"	43
Fairfax, Lord,	48
Fenn, Humphrey,	40, 45
Fenner, Dudley,	40
Field, John,	35, 36
Flavel, John,	70, 81, 86
Fleming, Robert,	95
"Form of Church Government,"	50, 60
Foxe, John,	27, 30
"Geneva Bible,"	27
Gibb, John,	120
Gilby, Anthony,	27, 31, 36
Gillespie, Alexander,	108
Gilpin, Bernard,	81
Gilpin, Richard,	81, 97
Glynne, John,	48
Goodman, Christopher,	27, 31, 60
Graham, William (Newcastle),	103
Graham, William (Liverpool),	110
Gratian,	18
Grindal, Edmund,	38
Hamilton, James,	108, 110
Hampden, John,	48
Hampton Court Conference,	44
Happy Union, The,	81
Harley, Sir Robert,	48
Harris, Howell,	101
Haselrig, Sir Arthur	48
Henderson, Alexander,	46
Henry, Matthew,	60, 74, 81, 83, 96
Henry, Philip,	70, 72
Hewley, Lady,	105, 108
Herle, Charles,	48, 59
Heyrick, Richard,	59
High Commission, Court of,	28, 38
Hildersham, Arthur,	40, 44
Hollis, Denzil,	48
Hooker, Richard,	37
Hooper, John,	24, 26
Howe, John,	70
Humphrey, Lawrence,	31
Hunter, Henry,	95
Hyde, Sir Edward,	69
Independents,	60, 80, 81, 92
Indulgence, The,	71
"Institution of a Christian Man, The,"	20
Irving, Edward,	104
Jack, Robert,	110
Jenkyn, William,	69
Jerment, George,	110

	PAGE
King, Peter,	79, 100
King, David,	110
"Kingdom of Christ, On the,"	23
Knollys, Sir Francis,	36
Knox, John,	25, 27, 31, 35
Lardner, Nathaniel,	91
Laud, William,	45, 46, 73
Leighton, Alexander,	45
Lever, Thomas,	31, 36
Levi, Leone,	108
Ley, John,	60
Lightfoot, John,	49
Liverpool, Mount Pleasant,	103
-- Oldham Street,	103
-- Rodney Street,	104
Lombard, Peter,	18
London, Canonbury,	95
— Crown Court,	95
— Glasshouse Street,	95
— London Wall,	95
— Peter Street,	95
— Regent Square,	104, 111
— Swallow Street,	95
"Lord Bishops none of the Lord's Bishops,"	45
Lorimer, Peter,	108
Love, Christopher,	64
Lowick,	98
M'Crie, Thomas,	108
MacFarlane, John,	110
M'Kerrow, William,	110
Manchester, Earl of,	48, 63
— Lloyd Street,	103
— St. Peter's,	104
Manton, Thomas,	69, 70
Marprelate Tracts,	40
Marsden, Jeremiah,	95
Marshall, Stephen,	46, 49
Martindale, Adam,	60
Maynard, Sir John,	48
Milton, John,	46, 58, 68

	PAGE
Monk, General,	67
Morpeth,	98, 112
Morrison, Robert,	109
Munro, Alexander,	108
Newcastle, Blackett Street,	98
— John Knox Church,	98
Newcomen, Matthew,	46
Nisbet, James,	108
Non-Jurors,	80
Oath, Et cetera,	47
— Ex officio,	39
Ogle, Luke,	97
Oldcastle, Sir John,	20
"Order of Wandsworth,"	35
Oswald,	16
Paget, John,	60
Palmer, Herbert,	49, 54
Pan-Presbyterian Council,	122
Parker, Matthew,	28
Patrick, St.,	17
Perkins, William,	40, 42
Pierce, James,	86
Poole, Matthew,	70
"Practice of Prelates,"	21
Precisians,	13
Presbyterian Church in England,	107
Presbyterian Church of England,	112
Preston, John,	42
Priestley, Joseph,	92, 93
Prynne, William,	45
Puleston, Lady,	73, 74
Puritans,	14
Pym, John,	48
Rainolds, John,	40, 42, 44
Relief Synod,	110
Remonstrance, The Grand,	47
Reynolds, Edward,	49
Ridley, Nicholas,	25, 26
Roborough, Henry,	48
Rowlands, Daniel,	101

	PAGE
Rule, Gilbert,	97
Rutherford, Samuel,	54
"Saints' Everlasting Rest, The,"	66
Salters' Hall Synod,	86, 95
Sampson, Thomas,	27, 31, 36
Sautree, William,	20
Savoy Conference,	69
Saybrook Platform,	61
Scots' Presbytery,	95
Seaman, Lazarus,	49, 69
Secession Church,	95
Secker, Thomas,	85
Sectaries,	14, 39
Separatists,	14, 30, 39
Sheldon, Gilbert,	69, 71
Sibbes, Richard,	42
Sion College,	59
Skinner, John,	120
Smectymnuus,	46
Snape, Edward,	40
Spenser, Edmund,	43
Spurstow, William,	46
Stafford,	96
Stamfordham,	98
Star Chamber,	28
Stewart, John,	110
Strickland, William,	36
Subscription Controversy,	86
Taylor, John,	91
Theodore of Tarsus,	17
Thorpe, William,	20
Travers, Walter,	36, 37, 40
Tuckney, Anthony,	49, 54
Turner, William,	31
Twisse, William,	48

	PAGE
Tyndale, William,	21
Udall, John	40, 41
United Presbyterians,	110
Vermigli (Peter Martyr)	23
"Vindication of Presbyterial Government,"	63
Wallis, John,	49, 54
Wandsworth, Presbytery of,	34, 35
Warrington Academy,	92
Warwick, Earl of,	48
Waugh, Alexander,	110
Wentworth, Sir Peter,	36
Wesley, John,	79, 99
Westminster Assembly,	48
Wharton, Lord,	48
Whitaker, William,	40
Whitby, Synod of,	17
White, John,	48, 99
Whitefield, George,	93, 100
Whitgift, John,	36, 38
Whittingham, William,	27, 60
Wilcox, Thomas,	36, 40
Williams, Daniel,	81
Williams, Peter,	101
Williams, William,	101
Wishart, William,	95
Worcester House Declaration,	69
Wycliffe, John,	19
Young, George,	110
Young, Thomas,	46
"Zion's Plea against the Prelacy,"	45

ABERDEEN UNIVERSITY PRESS.

www.ingramcontent.com/pod-product-compliance
Lightning Source LLC
Chambersburg PA
CBHW021940160426
43195CB00011B/1166